D1614906

The Irish Dancing
Cultural Politics and Identities, 1900–2000

The Irish Dancing
Cultural Politics and Identities
1900–2000

BARBARA O'CONNOR

CORK UNIVERSITY PRESS

First published in 2013 by
Cork University Press
Youngline Industrial Estate
Pouladuff Road, Togher
Cork, Ireland

British Library Cataloguing in Publication Data
A CIP catalogue record for this book is available from the British Library.

ISBN 978-1-78205-041-4

Typeset by Tower Books, Ballincollig, County Cork
Printed by Gutenberg Press, Malta

www.corkuniversitypress.com

Contents

To the memory of my mother and father,
Maeve and John

Acknowledgements

I started writing this book when I was working in the School of Communications at Dublin City University but it was only following retirement in 2011 that I found time to finish it. So it was substantially the intellectual environment provided by colleagues both within and outside the School that informed my work during those twenty-five years. I would particularly like to thank Farrell Corcoran, who in his leadership role as Head of School was instrumental in creating a supportive intellectual environment in which to conduct research. The intellectual generosity and enthusiasm of other colleagues is equally appreciated. Stimulating conversations with Stephanie McBride, Michael Cronin, Luke Gibbons, Des McGuinness and Paschal Preston in pubs and parties as well as the pulpits of the academy have been an enriching source of my thinking about Irish cultural history and politics. In this capacity too I would like to thank postgraduate researchers Teresa Breathnach and Sean O Seanchair, as well as Eamonn Slater and Stephanie Rains, National University of Ireland, Maynooth.

I would like to pay a special tribute to Bill Dorris for his collegiality and friendship as well as for praxis – that judicious combination of theory and practice. Not only was he ever ready to discuss theory but was also more than willing to repair to the corridor outside our adjacent offices to practice reel steps. As we hoofed and whooped the bemused passers-by may well have been prompted to ponder the sanity of academics.

The experience of the dancers themselves has made an invaluable contribution to this book. Indeed, it would not have been possible to write without their voices. Thanks to the set dancers, step dancers and ballroom dancers who shared so generously their thoughts and feelings with me. I hope I have done them justice on the page. While their names have been changed to respect anonymity I owe them an enormous debt of gratitude.

I would like to acknowledge, too, specific help from a number of colleagues, Pat Brereton, John Horgan and Colum Kenny for helpful suggestions or references; Dave Coleman, Senior Press Officer, Office of the Revenue Commissioners for information on the 'dance tax'; Teresa Breathnach for sharing her grandfather's newspaper article on jazz; Timothy G. McMahon, Marquette University for useful leads on early Oireachtas competitions (leads not yet pursued, I'm afraid!) and Harvey O'Brien, University College Dublin for information on the Mars ballroom.

I have also been the beneficiary of involvement with a dance research community, Dance Research Forum Ireland (DRFI) based in the University of Limerick whose members at the time, Catherine Foley, Orfhlaith Ní Bhriain, Olive Beecher, Victoria O'Brien, and Matts Melin were actively involved in developing a public profile for dance research in Ireland and who made me feel very welcome. I am, likewise, indebted to dance ethnographers Helena Wulff and Frank Hall for their writing and conversations on dance.

My gratitude to colleague and friend Elisabeth Klaus, Department of Communication, University of Salzburg, for the opportunity to teach at the University and to share ideas on dance with staff and students there.

My thanks to the staff of DCU library and to the Irish Traditional Music Archive for their efficiency and helpfulness over the years.

I am especially grateful to the staff of Cork University Press, particularly Maria O'Donovan, for their tireless professional efforts in bringing this book to publication.

Thanks to my friends Jonathan Bell for constant encouragement and for sourcing the cover image, Ann Connolly for checking image sources and some relatively unsuccessful 'assertiveness training', and my sister Lorna for chasing those last elusive references.

Finally, my gratitude to all my family and friends for their love and support.

CHAPTER ONE

The Irish Dancing
Cultural Politics and Identities

The theme of this volume, the role of dance in Irish cultural politics and identities in the twentieth century, can be book-ended by two dance events. The first, an Irish céilí and social event, was held in the Bloomsbury Hall in London on 31 October 1897, organised by the Gaelic League, at this time the main organisation for the promotion of cultural nationalism and for spearheading the Gaelic Revival in the late nineteenth and early twentieth centuries. The céilí, the first of its kind, was the outcome of efforts by League leaders to create an 'authentically' Irish dance canon that, in their view, would accurately reflect the ancient Irish nation and help to lay the cultural foundations for the establishment of an independent state in the future. The event can be seen as symbolic of the role dance was to play in generating a distinctive sense of Irish national identity. The second theatrical dance event, taking place almost one hundred years later, on 30 April 1994, at the Point Depot in Dublin, was a seven-minute step-dance routine as the interval act in the annual Eurovision song contest. The critical success of this act, with its two lead Irish-American dancers, Michael Flatley and Jean Butler, and a troupe of twenty-four Irish step dancers, led to the production of a full-scale music and dance show with its debut in the same venue in 1995. *Riverdance: The Show* went on to achieve extraordinary critical and commercial acclaim. With its spin-off products, four dance troupes in each major global region and its role as inspiration for new theatrical dance shows, it can be seen as a major contributor to Irish cultural industries and to the continuing association of Irishness with dance. Indeed, this is so much the case that 'Riverdancing' has become the generic term for Irish step dance in the USA.

These two events, illustrate the importance of dance in Irish cultural expression and its pivotal role in the formation of cultural identities at two key moments at either end of the century. This book engages with these two events, as well as other dance events, performances and discourses, in order to examine the ways in which cultural identities were constructed, maintained and altered through dance over the course of the century. Underlying the discussion throughout is the assumption that dance both reflects and produces society and culture. That dance reflects the social, cultural and political contexts within which it is performed and represented has long been attested to by sociologists and dance scholars alike (see, for example, Rust, 1969; Elias, 1978; Foucault, 1981; Bourdieu, 1984; Polhemus, 1993; Franko, 1995). Dancing individuals not only experience culture but they also actively produce it. In other words they 'mobilise culture for being, doing and feeling' (de Nora, 2000, p. 74).

Dance is tightly interwoven into the fabric of Irish culture and society. There has been a contentious claim that there was no dancing in Ireland until the coming of the Normans in the twelfth century. The origins of this belief, according to dance historian Breandán Breathnach (1977, p. 36), was that the two modern Irish words for dancing, 'rince' and 'damhsa', derive from the French and English language respectively and only began to appear in the early sixteenth century. Breathnach acknowledges that the assumption that dance was therefore absent from Irish culture before this time seems highly implausible, since dance constitutes part of the warp and weft of most, if not all, known cultures. However, what counts as dance and its functions within a society as well as its associated meanings and pleasures will vary according to the historical and geographical circumstances in which it is performed.

Broadly speaking, dance can be categorised into three analytically distinct forms of activity: dance as ritual performance, dance as a pastime or leisure activity, and dance as an art form. In tribal cultures dance is integrated into many aspects of daily life. It is believed to be efficacious in fighting wars or in bringing rain, as well as accompanying rites of passage such as birth, marriage and death. It is a form of ritualised movement and is inextricably linked to other domains of life, including the religious and the economic. Vestiges of dance as pre-Christian seasonal ritual can still be seen in events and practices such as Oíche Naomh Eoin/St John's Eve, Wren boys performing on St Stephen's Day, mumming, and the Maypole dance. There is an overall decline in many of these dance events, though both mumming and Wren boy activities have undergone a revival in recent years. Dance is still a very popular entertainment at weddings and is a good example of the blurring of dance as ritual and as a leisure activity.

Historical accounts attest to the popularity of dance as a pastime or leisure activity at least as far back as the seventeenth century, when travellers such as Arthur Young commented on the proclivity of the Irish poor for dancing, claiming that it was almost universal in every cabin (Young, 1892). From cabin to big house and from indoor to outdoor dancing, it continued as a popular recreational activity throughout the following century. During the first half of the twentieth century it could be safely said that it was the most common leisure activity for the majority of young people and the dance hall was the most common place for meeting prospective marriage partners. Indeed the role of leisure, as outlined by Victor Turner (1982, p. 37), is equally fitting to dance being characterised by:

> freedom from forced chronologically regulated rhythms of factory and office and a chance to recuperate and enjoy natural biological rhythms again . . . It is, furthermore, freedom to transcend social structural limitations, freedom to play . . . leisure can be hard or exacting, subject to rules and routines even more stringent than those at the workplace, but because they are optional, voluntary, they are part of an individual's freedom, of his growing self-mastery, even self-transcendence.

Testimony to the continuing importance of social and recreational dance is the assumption that most readers of this book will have had some kind of personal experience of dance, whether at the wedding, tennis hop, parish hall, disco, rave or club. And it is likely that this experience will be linked to some kind of emotional response, though not all will be as positive as Turner suggests above. While some have the urge to dance whenever they hear a particular tune, others are reluctant dancers and complain of having 'two left feet'. Whatever one's personal orientation to dance, it continues to be an important part of the leisure landscape into the twenty-first century.

Dance as an art form has also played a key role in Irish society over the course of the twentieth century, whether as 'high' art (e.g. the Irish National Ballet) or popular entertainment (e.g. *Riverdance*). Early in the century theatre dance formed an important part of programming at the Abbey Theatre under the stewardship of Yeats and Lady Gregory. In mid-century we saw the opening of the Irish National Ballet by Joan Denise Moriarty. Towards the end of the century there was a proliferation of modern-dance companies. Competitive dancing of all kinds adds another dimension to dance as entertainment. And apart from live theatre shows, dance was well represented in the broadcast media as art and entertainment. Perhaps one of the most curious and quirky aural representations was when listeners were treated to the sound of Irish step dance on radio in Din Joe's (Denis Fitzpatrick) show *Take the Floor*, on Radio Éireann in the early 1960s. Representations of dance in literature, film and television abound and some have become iconic. One of the most electrifying and powerful moments in Brian Friel's play *Dancing at Lughnasa* is when the Mundy sisters, who are baking bread, suddenly break into a wild dance, leaping, hopping, twirling and shouting around the kitchen of their Donegal cottage when they hear a lively Irish tune on the radio. With the advent of reality television, the last decade has also seen a variety of television dance shows, such as the BBC show *Strictly Come Dancing*, RTÉ's *Ballet Chancers* and *Celebrity Jigs and Reels*, and TG4's *An Jig Gig*.

Dance too has been a popular trope in both the political rhetoric and representation of Irishness. Dancing 'colleens' smile out at us from the images in the British press accompanying reports of the Irish village, Ballymaclinton, at the British–Franco exhibition in White City, London, in 1908. These dancing Irish women symbolised the positive role they could play in saving the Irish within the British imperial structure at a time of agitation for Home Rule (see Chapter Two). Dancing imagery continued to play a part in the political symbolism of the post-colonial era. This is perhaps most famously illustrated in the apocryphal phrase 'comely maidens dancing at the crossroads', which is attributed to Eamon de Valera's St Patrick's Day radio speech of 1943. The actual speech, reported in the *Irish Press* the following day, did refer to the 'laughter of comely maidens' but made no reference to dance. Despite this, the phrase made its way into popular parlance and has remained as a term of mockery of de Valera's aspirational vision of Ireland as a rural idyll. More recently, Mary Robinson in her inaugural speech as President of Ireland in 1990, issued an invitation to the Irish worldwide to 'come dance with me in Ireland'. The lines quoted from the fourteenth-century poem were at once an invitation to the Irish diaspora to regard Ireland as their home, a symbol of an inclusiveness that she aspired to achieve in her term as president, as well as an acknowledgement of the potential contribution of the diaspora to the modern Irish nation.

From these broad brushstrokes it is clear that dance was an integral part of Irish life as ritual, as leisure, and as art and entertainment over the course of the twentieth century. Despite its ubiquity as a form of cultural expression and representation, it has been relatively neglected as an object of study either within Irish cultural sociology or Irish cultural studies. Over the years, I have trawled through many of the classic sociological and anthropological texts ever hopeful of finding substantial accounts of dancing in its social context only to find the occasional tangential reference or a brief functional account of its role in a specific community, the latter useful but not sufficiently revealing. In some ways the relative invisibility of analytic accounts of dance in Irish culture is not surprising, since dance has been relatively neglected as an object of interest within cultural sociology generally. Jane C. Desmond (1998, pp. 154–5) maintains that dance 'remains a greatly undervalued and under-theorised arena of bodily discourse. Its practice and its scholarship are with rare exception, marginalised within the academy'. She attributes some of this neglect to the 'continuing rhetorical association of bodily expressivity with non-dominant groups' such as women and minority ethnic groups. She points out the failure of scholarship thus far:

> Given the amount of information that public display of movement provides, its scholarly isolation in the realms of technical studies in kinesics, aesthetics, sports medicine and some cross-cultural communications studies is both remarkable and lamentable. (p. 156)

Desmond goes on to urge scholars to acquire the skills necessary to ask and answer pertinent questions about the role of dance in culture; questions such as who dances with whom, when and where, and to what end? Even more neglected in sociological accounts is social/recreational dance (see Ward, 1997). And yet another challenge to dance scholarship identified by Janet Wolff (foreword to Adair, 1992, p. xi) is the absence of a macro perspective within cultural sociology:

> dance only appears in small-scale, empirical studies of particular companies or groups of dancers: providing little in the way of a

more complex understanding of how dance operates in the social sphere.

The relative absence of analytic accounts of dance in Irish society can also be attributed to culturally specific factors that are linked to the historical development of Irish sociology as a discipline. I have argued elsewhere (O'Connor, 1987) that there was a dearth of cultural analysis in early Irish sociology. This was partially explained by the fact that many of the first-generation sociologists were trained in the USA within the positivist tradition, which led to the consequent hegemony of quantitative methods as the only legitimate (i.e. 'scientific') mode of social enquiry. Since reliance was placed on large-scale surveys to acquire sociological knowledge of Irish society, the climate was not conducive to the qualitative research that was often the most appropriate to the analysis of culture. The analysis of popular culture tended to be monopolised by those employing interpretive methods such as the anthropologist, historian or literary critic/journalist. Irish sociology also tended to be issue/problem-based and policy-oriented, due in some measure to the pivotal role of the Catholic Church in developing the discipline in Irish universities. Dance, when it was discussed at all, was framed in terms of a problem within a functionalist analysis; for example, the dearth of leisure activities such as dances in rural areas was seen as a contributing factor to the large-scale emigration of its young people. And, finally and crucially, dance had been neglected because it deals with the body and with sexuality, areas of enquiry monopolised until relatively recently 'by doctors, theologians, bishops and priests' (Inglis and Liston, 2003, p. 3).

Irish dance is not lost to scholarship, however, and, sociological neglect aside, there are a number of excellent studies from historical, ethnochoreological or anthropological perspectives, from which I will draw extensively throughout this volume. Each of these studies presents a range of foci and sets of questions germane to their discipline. Breandán Breathnach's now classic work is probably the first historical account of dance, providing an excellent overview of the role of dance in Ireland from 1700 to the 1980s, and has become the primary source of much data for subsequent writing on dance. Helen Brennan's book *The Story of Irish Dance* (1999) is also an excellent overview of dancing in Ireland with the emphasis on traditional dancing during the twentieth century and including rich ethnographic material from Connemara in particular. John

Cullinane's series of six volumes provides very valuable information on traditional dance and is particularly valued for its detailed data on a range of aspects of traditional Irish dance, from dancing costumes to dancing among the Irish diaspora. Cullinane's access to documentary archives from An Coimisiún le Rincí Gaelacha provides unique data on the major role played by this institution in the promotion and regulation of traditional Irish dance. I found Susan Gedutis's (2004) ethnographically rich book exploring Boston's 'golden era' of Irish music and dance during the 1940s invaluable in gaining an understanding of dance among a section of the Irish diaspora. Helena Wulff's (2007) book *Dancing at the Crossroads: Memory and Mobility in Ireland* was also a source of valuable information on traditional dance in Ireland post-*Riverdance* in the wider context of tradition, memory and cosmopolitanism. Other books, though not of direct relevance, either because of the period under review or the kind of dance in question, have provided a useful background context. These include Mary Friel's (2004) historical account of social dancing in County Wexford in the nineteenth century as well as Deirdre Mulrooney's (2006) book on dance and physical theatre.

Each of these books makes a welcome and distinctive contribution to scholarship on Irish dance, to which I hope to add by complementing and developing some of the themes already addressed by these scholars. I adopt a critical cultural studies approach which, following Desmond's (1998, p. 161n.) definition, necessitates the investigation of the links between social, economic and political power with the production/performance and representation of dance in an Irish cultural context. The discussion is embedded in a broadly sociological frame and also draws on cultural theories of dance as well as comparative empirical research from other cultures, where appropriate.

Partly thematic, partly chronological, this exploration of dance emerges out of my own enjoyment of dancing as well as a broader interest in movement, travel and the body in society. It comprises seven chapters, each of which addresses a particular form of cultural identity: national, ethnic, gender, social class, postmodern and global. Most chapters are devoted to a specific identity formation, while issues of gender and social class are interwoven into most chapters. Apart from the last chapter, on stage/theatrical dance, the book's main focus is on social/recreational dance.

Since the concepts of cultural identity and cultural politics are the two key themes in this volume, it is useful at this stage to outline what I mean by them and their value in the discussion of dance in Irish culture. Broadly speaking, identity can be seen to imply a sense of who we are, and of how we place ourselves in society. We categorise ourselves and others in terms of personal traits and characteristics, constructing a sense of personal identity. We also categorise in terms of where we come from, building a sense of ethnic or national identity, or whether we are male or female, in this case building a sense of gender identity. Often mistakenly categorised as a static concept, identity is best regarded as an active and continuous process in which identifications shift and change over time amongst specific individuals and groups in society. The sense of cultural identity as both continuous and significant is captured in Stuart Hall's view of it as a 'production', which is 'never complete, always in process, and always constituted within, not outside, representation' (Hall, 1990, p. 222). Snape (2009, p. 299) also sees the interlinking of action, symbolism and identity in claiming that 'identity is not something simply acquired but is constituted by action; it is a symbolic realm within which the performative enactment of identity occurs'. In other words we act out who we think we are or want to be and how we want others to see us. It is also a relative term in that it is dependent not only on self-categorisation but also on one's reciprocal categorisation by others.

Identity formation, frequently seen as an exclusively cognitive process – a mental category for labelling self and others – is also a bodily one. It is the interaction between mind and body that generates identity. When we place dance within the broader context of bodily mobility, we can see the link between dance and identity formation. Dance is influenced by other 'techniques of the body' (Mauss, 1973 [1934]) or types of gestures, postures and movement styles that develop within a particular group. Desmond (1998, p. 54), for instance, points to the strong link between the body, dance and identity and suggests that '[b]y enlarging our studies of bodily "texts" to include dance in all its forms . . . we can further our understanding of how social identities are signalled, formed and negotiated through bodily movement'.

Further, by looking at dance she claims that:

[W]e can see enacted on a broad scale, and in codified fashion, socially constituted and historically specific attitudes toward the body in general, toward specific social groups' usage of the body in particular, and about the relationships among variously marked bodies, as well as social attitudes toward the use of space and time. (p. 157)

Culture itself is 'an arena of power struggles and conflict as well as a basis for social unity and cohesion' (Tovey and Share, 2000, p. 283), so that cultural politics is endemic. As to the cultural politics of dance, the same kind of embodied approach can be applied as to cultural identities. The body according to Teresa de Lauretis (1986, p. 11) is 'the very site of material inscription of the ideological, the ground where socio-political determinations take hold and are realised'. If we extend this observation to dance we can see how cultural identities and cultural politics are, in fact, two sides of the same coin, since politics are inscribed in and performed by dancing bodies. The cultural politics of dance operates at the micro-level of the individual dancer through the negotiation of dance norms and practices with others and at a macro-level by organisations and institutions who can determine the predominant meanings of dance and regulate and control dance practice.

Having established a relationship between dance, the body and identities, what are the factors that influence the 'techniques of the body' and of the dancing body over space and time? At the most basic level, characteristic ways of moving the body are generally adapted to suit the habitual movement requirements of the body in everyday life. This results in both cross-cultural commonalities and differences in bodily mobility. For instance peasant societies may develop specific ways of moving that are in line with the physical requirements of working the land. This relationship between physique and environment is beautifully illustrated in John Berger's (1980) essay, 'The Suit and the Photograph'. The suit(s) in question are those worn by a group of French rural workers in a late nineteenth-century photograph. Berger observes how the suit, developed for urban businessmen, looks ill-fitting on the bodies of the French peasant. This is so, he concludes, because the body shape of the peasant has developed from 'techniques of the body' used in hard physical labour as opposed to the body shapes developed by the sedentary techniques of the urban businessman. The differential body appearance and shape influenced by lifestyles noted by Berger can be observed equally clearly in a contemporary context when we take note of the countryman's walk in the city, the toned body of the gym user or athletics trainer, or the fake tan of the Celtic Tiger cubs.[1]

Distinctive movement styles are also associated with specific cultures and ethnicities, giving rise to dance stereotypes. Stuart Hall (2003) reminds us that these stereotypes are not necessarily true or false but can be given a positive or negative spin according to the political interests involved in their attribution. Some cultures are seen to possess an innate love of dance and/or a natural dancing ability; Latin and African cultures, for example, are regarded as having natural rhythm and expressiveness, while northern European cultures are seen as more challenged in terms of bodily movement. The Irish dancing body too has been the object of positive and negative stereotypes. The perceived proclivity of the Irish for dance can be constructed either positively as in tourist imagery, where dancing is a component in the broader stereotype of a fun-loving people renowned for their music, drinking and 'craic', or negatively as in the colonial discourse of a work-shy people with an excessive interest in amusements and thereby unfit for self-governance.

The predominant stereotype of the Irish dancing body for much of the twentieth century has been a negative one of a rigid upper body where nothing moves but the feet, frequently seen as a reflection of a repressed and constrained body, fearful of touch and sensuality. Commentators on dance frequently attribute this bodily 'habitus' (Bourdieu, 1984) to the burden of oppression under either colonial or Roman (religious) rule. In this scenario, the dominant role of the Catholic Church in the education of children and the consequent imposition of negative attitudes towards the body is sometimes seen as causal. The Irish body style is also seen as apologetic (Keane, cited in Mulrooney, 2006, p. 199). While extremely erect posture is commonly associated with Irish step dance, a Dance Officer in Belfast decries its absence in Irish postural style: 'We slouch, you stand and your shoulders hunch, your hands in your pockets. Especially men in bars. It's a lazy way of standing, a lazy way of sitting' (quoted in Wulff, 2005, p. 48). Negativity has also been associated with the function of dance in Irish culture. Fintan O'Toole (1997, pp. 145–6), for example, suggests that for much of the twentieth century the Irish dancing body has been dysfunctional, in the sense that dance has been used as a means of escape rather than communication:

> In most cultures, dancing is an expression of the community, a ritual of togetherness. To go to a dance is to participate in a place. Through dancing, the private – sexual desire, courtship, family relations – is played out as public display. The gap between the personal and the social is narrowed. But in Ireland, for most of the 20th Century at least, dancing was often about avoiding the community, even of avoiding communication. It became a private activity, an act, not of communication or expression, but of escape.

However accurate and general these observations on Irish movement and dancing are, it is important not to reify 'the Irish body' as something immutable and monolithic. Writer Elizabeth Bowen reminds us that particular corporeal styles are differentiated within Irish culture. The Anglo–Irish, in her opinion, had a distinctive orientation towards dance. Reminiscing on her attendance at dance classes as a child, she (1942, p. 92) muses on what her Austrian dance teacher might have thought of the Anglo-Irish pupils, of which Bowen was one:

> I do not know what she thought of us Anglo-Irish children, from whom the austere grace of one race had been bred away and who still missed the naive, positive gracelessness of another. I would say that in general, the Anglo–Irish do not make good dancers; they are too spritely and conscious; they are incapable of one kind of trance or of being sensuously impersonal. And, for the formal, pure dance they lack the formality; about their stylishness (for they have stylishness) there is something impromptu, slightly disorderly.

While trying to avoid essentialising the Irish body, it is vital, nonetheless, to acknowledge the significance of national cultures in producing distinctive techniques of the body that reflect specific social and cultural conditions at any particular point in time. This book opens with a consideration of just how distinctively Irish techniques of the body were produced through national discourses on dance at the beginning of the twentieth century. Chapters Two and Three address the role of the dancing body in the construction and maintenance of national identity, from the Cultural Revival in the 1890s through to the 1930s. The main questions addressed in this context are, what were considered to be the most appropriate dance forms and styles for Irish people at this time? Were certain styles forbidden? Who took responsibility for putting these in place? And what were the strategies used to do so? In these two chapters the emphasis is placed on the institutions and organisations who were instrumental in shaping and regulating the individual dancing body. Both chapters foreground the power of national institutions – the Gaelic League in Chapter Two, the Catholic Church and the state itself in Chapter Three – to shape the development of Irish dance during this period. Chapter Two examines the ways in which dance became a key signifier in the construction of national identity and traces the trajectory of dance as an inherent part of the project of culturalism nationalism. This project was inextricably intertwined with the establishment of the Gaelic League in 1893, the League being the main organisation to set up cultural values and norms to be achieved by the Irish nation and the aspirational state. The chapter examines the context in which the new canon of Irish dance was established; the revival of folk dancing in Europe and the USA; the legacy of colonial discourses of the body against which distinctive and 'authentically' Irish techniques of the body should be established. The chapter also engages with the internal politics of the League in the process of developing the Irish dance canon, through the choice of dances considered to be authentically Irish, through the establishment of rules and protocols of competition dancing at feiseanna, the establishment of dance schools, as well as other aspects of dance training and regulation.

While acknowledging the importance of national culture as a frame of reference for investigating dance, it is also crucial to remember the great variability in body techniques and movement regimes that develop within particular groups or categories within the society. Gender, for instance, is a crucial structural variable in learning and performing specific 'techniques of the body'. In this regard Polhemus (1998, p. 176) refers to the universality of the gender dimension of dance in proposing that:

> culture in its broadest sense is embodied in the form of physical culture and this in turn is stylised and schematised in the form of dance. However, while this process itself may be unrelated to gender, the end results always are: the cultural reality which, for example, Masai (etc.) men express in their dance will be a different

cultural reality than that which Masai (etc.) women express in their dance.

Social class and status hierarchies are also expressed and reproduced through dance, with distinctions constantly being drawn between what is considered appropriate and inappropriate dancing behaviour for a particular class, or what dance venues are considered acceptable or forbidden. It is suggested in Chapters Two and Three that both gender and social class discourses were intertwined in the emerging discourse on dance in the Cultural Revival era. Chapter Two addresses issues of gender by examining how different styles of dance were encouraged for men and women through published dance manuals and by exploring the gradual feminisation of step-dance teaching and performance between the 1890s and 1920s.

Chapter Three continues with the theme of dance and national identity in the period between 1922 and 1935. It investigates the role of key cultural players in consolidating the nation through the cultivation of dancing bodies that were shaped to reflect the ideal body politic of the newly established state. The attempts to develop that ideal body resulted in a prolonged struggle between the forces of tradition and modernity in relation to public dance practice, the alliance on the side of tradition comprising the Gaelic League, the Catholic Church and the state. The emphasis in this chapter is on the control and regulation of dance and the 'moral panic' that developed in public discourses on dance. The discussion is situated within the context of the increasing restrictions on popular leisure during the 1920s, and particularly the censorship of 'foreign' cultural imports, including publications, films and dances, during this decade. The concern with 'threatening mobilities' (Cresswell, 2006, p. 57) continued into the 1930s and became more intensive with the attempts to control the increasingly popular modern dance – what had by this time come to be known as jazz dancing. The Anti-Jazz Campaign was established and its lobbying finally led to state regulation of public dancing with the introduction of the Public Dance Halls Act in 1935. The chapter also suggests that there was a clearly visible gender dynamic operating within the broader dance discourses of tradition and modernity which could be traced to a binary discourse on women in which they were seen to be simultaneously dangerous and vulnerable within the public dancing space.

Individual dancing bodies, however, are not merely reflective of the social order, but are simultaneously active agents in the making of that order. They are powerful and productive in and of themselves or, in Desmond's (1998, p. 158) words, '[s]ocial relations are both enacted and produced through the body, and not merely inscribed upon it'. Cresswell (2006, p. 58) too acknowledges the dialectical relationship between the normative and experiental in bodily movement: 'While it is clear that bodily movement is a form of meaning-making that is crucial to the production of cultural and social norms, it is also clear that bodies express already existing normative ideals.' So while societal institutions may have the power to regulate the dancing body through internalisation of dance norms, dancing bodies have the power to either reproduce, resist or challenge these same norms. Rituals of the 'carnivalesque' (Bakhtin, 1984) attest to the bodily capacity for transgressive and rebellious resistance through participation in dance and other carnival rituals. Responses are not mutually exclusive and, as noted by Novack (1995, p. 181) the dancing body may both reflect and resist cultural values simultaneously.

Power then is not simply a regulatory one but produces a variety of meanings and pleasures for dancers, individual and collective, intrinsic and extrinsic, kinaesthetic and cognitive. Indeed the three concepts of power, meanings and pleasures, while analytically distinct, are generally integrated in dance performance. As Mauss, one of the early cultural sociologists, observed, bodily movement is always subject to the human psychosocial realm of meaning production (Mauss, 1973 [1934]). Bourdieu (1990) also acknowledges the intertwining of power, meanings and pleasure in the body. Any understanding of dance in culture calls, therefore, for an analytic approach that captures dancing experiences including the meanings and pleasures of dance performance itself.

This approach is adopted in Chapter Four, which focuses on the power, meanings and pleasures of ballroom dancing in the 1940s and 1950s. Drawing on documentary sources and interview data with women, the discussion revolves around the negotiation of new forms of gender identities. It is proposed that the building of ballrooms in towns around Ireland from the 1930s on provided dancers, and female dancers especially, with a 'utopian space' of romance. Even though dance was an equally popular leisure activity with men and women, it is argued that the latter were more immersed in the ideology of romance. It is suggested that the dance hall provided a public space with a romantic ambience in which romantic activity could be performed. It is claimed furthermore that the discourse of romance was intertwined with discourses of modernity and consumption and that women had a distinctive relationship to both. However, I also highlight some of the displeasures of dancing and suggest that the 'utopian space' provided in the ballrooms was not without its contradictions.

Social dance forms have changed over the course of the century with a tendency for one style to become dominant in a particular decade or era. For example, communal dancing (symbolising community) was to a large extent replaced by couple dancing (symbolising the nuclear family) and it, in turn, was replaced by free-style dancing (symbolising individualism). However, there are also dance revivals and the same dance form may produce different meanings and pleasures at different points in time. This issue is addressed in Chapter Five, on set dancing, which at one time was the most popular dance form in rural Ireland but which had gone into decline in the 1930s and regained national popularity in the 1980s. The discussion here is based on conversations with set dancers in Dublin in the mid-1990s. While some of the meanings and pleasures of set dance have remained constant, it is argued that the economic, social and cultural changes in Irish society between the 1930s and the 1990s resulted in new meanings and pleasures coalescing around it. Dancers' gratifications, I suggest, derived from their living in an urban setting in an era of high modernity or postmodernity. It is contended that set dancing for these participants was a sign of their quest for a sense of 'community' in a time and place where traditional ideas of community were increasingly difficult to realise due to the dis-embedding of local cultures and increasing individualisation within Irish society. The interview data suggests that set dancing provided a sense of community created through the dance. Some dancers associated the forms of contact, friendship and communication experienced in dancing with rural life and folk culture. However, I also suggest that this longing for 'home' was contradictory and that the dancers also expressed an ambivalence about their nostalgic desire for the rural idyll. In doing so they exhibited a reflexive self-awareness of what Whelan (1996, p. 13) refers to as the 'doppelganger of rural life', and were glad to escape from the gravity of tradition associated with it and have the opportunity to enjoy the relative independence, anonymity and freedom of the city.

While a historical perspective is crucial to an understanding of identity formation through dance, so too is a geographical one. For example Gregson and Rose (2000, p. 434) believe that the notion of performance 'is indeed crucial for a critical human geography concerned to understand the construction of social identity, social difference, and social power relations, and the way space might articulate all of these'. Cresswell, too (2006, p. 71), acknowledges the importance of the spatial dimension of movement in general and sees 'particular sets of associations between ways of moving and real and imagined spaces and places' and that there is a value in 'thinking of mobilities as produced within social, cultural and, most importantly, geographical contexts'. Other scholars (Crouch, 2007; Silk, 2007) claim that when this type of analysis is applied to dance performance it can provide insights into the creation, control and meaning of leisure spaces.

The geographical/space and historical/time merge in Chapter Six, which is devoted to the role of dance for the Irish diaspora and specifically the ways in which Irish ethnic identity has been and continues to be reproduced through dance. Throughout the twentieth century emigration was a constant feature of Irish life, resulting in the spread of Irish dance and music to many parts of the world, especially to Britain, North America, Australia and New Zealand. Dance acted as a distinct marker of Irish cultural identity, both for the emigrants themselves and for subsequent generations to whom Irish cultural practices have been transmitted. It operates in two ways. Firstly, it constructs a sense of ethnic community in their place of residence where they meet and socialise through music and dance and transmit knowledge of tunes and dances from one generation to the next. Secondly, it is a means of connecting them to their Irish home. For the Irish emigrant, the home place is elsewhere; it is 'imagined' in terms of both the past and the future – the past as a form of cultural memory and the future as a desire to return to the homeland. The themes of cultural purity and authenticity, the subject of Chapters Two and Three, are addressed again here in the context of the emergence of hybrid or hyphenated Irish cultures abroad.

Chapter Seven, on *Riverdance* and post-*Riverdance* stage shows, the only chapter to focus exclusively on stage dance, addresses the issue of Irish identity towards the end of the century. Using *Riverdance* as an example of a dance product in a global cultural economy, the chapter examines the ways in which a number of scholars have interpreted the kinds of cultural identities represented by the show's narrative and choreography. It also draws on discussions with a number of young dancers in a post-*Riverdance* show to explore the ways in which the dancers themselves negotiate their cultural identities. The correspondences and divergences between these accounts indicate that the sense of Irishness reflected in and constitued by shows like *Riverdance* is complex and contradictory. At one level, it is argued, it could be seen to construct a global identity that was strongly influenced by the globalisation process, leading to a branding of Irishness that was strategic, depoliticised and commodified. On the other hand, it was arguably a source of rejuvenation for traditional Irish culture and a sign of a confident society that was coming of age, proud of its achievements on the world stage.

The thematic diversity of these seven chapters made the choice of the book's title challenging. I had considered two options, *Irish Dance* and *Dance in Ireland*. However, neither of these could easily capture the content. While most of the chapters deal with 'traditional' Irish dance forms, either step dance (in both a performance and recreational context) or set dance, Chapter Three engages with ballroom dancing, which does not originate in, nor is generally regarded as, Irish. However, whether dancing is categorised as Irish or not is dependent not just on the perceived origins of the dance genre itself, but on other factors such as the location, the music, the ethnic origins of the people who attend or, indeed, the 'techniques of the body' that have an Irish cultural valence. The discussion in Chapter Six on dance and diaspora also led me away from the *Dance in Ireland* choice, as it engages with dance practice elsewhere, albeit dance which is nonetheless regarded as Irish, either because of an Irish clientele (emigrants or first or second-generation Irish) or the music played (for example the Irish–American music played in the Boston dance halls in the 1940s and 1950s). I finally opted for *The Irish Dancing* as the most appropriate, since the main narrative in the chapters that follow is about the changing character of their cultural identities as danced by the Irish over the course of the twentieth century.

CHAPTER TWO

The Body Politic

Dance and National Identity

There is a scene in the film *Some Mother's Son* (1996), set in Northern Ireland during the recent 'Troubles', in which a classroom of young girls are practising their step dancing. Their rhythmic foot movements are intercut with the movements of IRA volunteers preparing to launch an attack on a British army convoy. The close-up montage of dancing feet and loading weapons to the sound of Irish dance music builds to a crescendo and sets up a visual link between Irish step dance and nationalism. This link is the theme of this chapter, which traces some of the key elements and processes in its making. The chapter addresses the question of how dance became such a powerful marker of national identity in the late nineteenth and early twentieth centuries and outlines the efforts made during these decades to develop a canon of 'authentic' and 'traditional' dance that was seen as distinctively Irish. It is argued that the Irish dancing body was shaped in such a way that it could adequately reflect the body politic of the nascent nation-state.

National and Folk Cultures

The connection between dance and nationalism, militant or otherwise, is well rehearsed in the literature on Irish dance. The Gaelic Revival, the term now given to the cultural nationalist movement that emerged in Ireland towards the end of the nineteenth century, was characterised by the promotion of what were widely perceived to be distinctively Irish cultural practices. This was regarded as necessary preparation for the overturning of colonial British rule and the formation of an independent Irish state.

Irish revivalists were not alone in their concern to revitalise 'traditional' national culture and their project can be seen as part of a broader movement to promote the unique cultural heritage of many of the newly formed and emerging European nation-states. The intertwining of culture and politics in this way is well captured in the historian Benedict Anderson's (1983) concept of a national 'imagined community'. The community is imagined in the sense that bonds are created between members of this entity even though they do not know each other and for the most part will never meet. These bonds are established through the use of distinctive cultural symbols and practices such as language use, religious practice as well as other pursuits such as dance and sport. Indeed, for Anderson it was frequently the cultural element that preceded and gave birth to the political. Ireland seems to be a case in point, since the Gaelic League, the primary organisation of the Cultural Revival movement, was founded in 1893 almost thirty years before the establishment of the independent state.

League members were strongly influenced by European thinkers on the connection between culture and politics and in particular on the role of culture in the struggle for political independence. According to Mo Meyer (1995, p. 29), the 'educated Irish elite – poets, writers, artists, historians, philosophers and folklorists' who founded the League knew of and participated in the international debates of the day. The philosophy and policies of the League were strongly influenced by German linguistics and by the theories of Johann Herder, Kuno Meyer and Wilhelm von Humboldt. The connection between culture and nation was strongly developed in Herder's writing, believing as he did that each nation had a unique spirit that was expressed through modes of communication such as language and music as well as techniques of the body such as gesture, movement and dance. This unique spirit was captured in 'folk' culture, practised mostly by rural peasants, who were regarded as closer to nature and uncorrupted by modernity. Herder's analysis, however, presents something of a paradox. Its 'intrinsic dilemma' as identified by Natasha Casey being that (2002, p. 19):

> the folk are enchanting to those already corrupted by society's
> modernizing forces as they represent a connection to idealizations
> of the past when life was less 'complicated'. However, the folk are
> also patently uncivilised, compared to those living in the modern,
> though corrupt, world.

The tension identified in Herder's writing between the folk, seen as the bearers of tradition, and those who embraced modernity and innovation was to become strongly evident in the development of a distinctively Irish dance canon and was to re-emerge at various times throughout the twentieth century in discourses on dance. Brennan (1999, p. 31) identifies this tension and observes that the attempt to create the new canon of Irish dance was 'in essence, a cultural civil war with dance as the arena of combat'. Whatever the contradictions inherent in the philosophical discussions of folk culture, the linking of the 'folk' with 'tradition' was to become a cornerstone of the work of Irish Cultural Revivalists. Hobsbawm and Ranger (1983) have noted that not only were traditional/folk practices harnessed to projects of cultural nationalism in the late nineteenth century but they were often invented as 'traditional' practices. They coined the term 'invention of tradition', which refers, as the name implies, to a process whereby newly invented practices are presented as having a long history within a culture. Snape (2009, p. 298) points to the symbolic potential of folk dance and sees it changing from a practice being enjoyed for its own sake to 'a conscious symbolic act, representational of something beyond its immediate occurrence', and in this case of cultural nationalism. There is ample evidence of the 'invention of tradition' in the development of the new Irish dance canon.

Ireland was not alone in harnessing folk cultural practice, including dance, to the project of cultural nationalism (e.g. see Abrahams, 1993 and Feintuch, 2001). Indeed it could be argued that the emphasis on ethnic/national cultural differences was part of the logic of the play of the universal and particular within the development of nation-states (Wallerstein, 1991). But while there may have been a common theme of nationalism running through many cultural movements in the early twentieth century, 'the precise nature of the relationship between folk dance and national identity remains indeterminate and differs between countries' (Snape, 2009, p. 298). The creation of a national canon of Irish dance at the turn of the twentieth century must be understood, therefore, in terms of the wider historical, political and cultural context in which it occurred. What follows is an attempt to sketch in some of the key influences on the shaping of the Irish dancing body in line with the body politic at this time by examining how the Irish body was constructed under British colonial rule and how, when that rule was overturned, nationalists both mimicked and resisted colonial stereotypes. It is argued further that both colonial and nationalist constructions of the Irish body were underpinned by deep-seated gender and social-class discourses.

Dance, Colonialism and the Irish Body

British colonial rule in Ireland was a crucial part of the context in which the national canon of dance emerged. As already indicated, the *Zeitgeist* of the late nineteenth century was one of cultural nationalism, and the objective of those involved in the Gaelic Revival movement was to revive the Irish language, customs and folkways of 'traditional' Ireland, which were perceived to have been obliterated by the colonists. They envisaged a reclaiming of a culture regarded as distinctive, pure and authentic. Popular publications of the time attest to this process (see figs 1 and 2). It is against this backdrop of colonial relations between Ireland and Britain that the symbolism of the Irish ethnic body must be understood during these decades.

For centuries the Irish body had been defined, as in colonial discourse generally, in opposition to the British. While the latter were represented as upright (physically and morally), as hardworking, adult and reasonable, the Irish, in contrast, were portrayed as feckless, childlike, lazy and overfond of passing their time in drinking, playing music and dancing. The abiding colonial image of the Irishman from the 1860s was the ape-like cartoon figure of *Punch* magazine. Liz Curtis's (1984) insightful historical account traces this simian physiognomy, posture and demeanour to the combined effects of two events in Britain at this time. One was the publication of Darwin's theory of evolution, specifically that aspect of the theory which proposed a 'missing link' between the ape and the Englishman, the latter being considered as the pinnacle of the evolutionary process. The Irishman, placed much lower down the evolutionary scale, was believed to be that 'missing link'. The second significant event was the Fenian uprising of 1867 in which the rebels were represented as less than human, belligerent, irrational and violent. George Cruikshank's pictorial representation of the Irish provides ample evidence of Curtis's claims.

Another dominant colonial motif of the body in the early twentieth century was the 'white man's body' (an idealised British male body) promoted by notables such as Baden-Powell, founder of the Boy Scout Movement. Powell's writings on the 'white man's body' reveal his fears that venereal disease, intermarriage between races and declining birthrates were endangering Britain's imperial power. His intention in founding the Scouts, therefore, was to restore imperial success by developing athleticism, self-sufficiency and chivalry in Britain's boys and young men. Amongst other things this entailed cultivating the stance of the 'white man', who was imagined as tall, muscular, with eyes straight ahead and body at attention and who could be clearly distinguished from 'the man', the imperial subject who, according to Powell, wished to emulate the white/British man (see Enloe, 1989, p. 50).

It may seem curious that, while the representation of the Irish male body at the beginning of the twentieth century was extremely negative, the opposite was true of the representation of the Irish female body. Since imperial exhibitions were one of the main displays of the range of ethnicities within the British empire, they are a useful source of information. I draw on evidence from one such exhibition, the British–Franco exhibition held in White City, London, in 1908, to support my argument. Amid this display of cultures from all corners of the empire was the 'Irish village' of Ballymaclinton, peopled by hardworking, clean and chaste Irish women who also gave exhibitions of Irish dance at set times over the duration of the exhibition (see fig. 3). Annie Coombes' (1994, p. 207) analysis of the exhibition examines the origins of these positive images of women and places them within the socio-political context of the time. She claims that the 'Irish colleens' (as the press referred to them) served to solidify a whole set of ideologies. She draws on the book, *Women of All Nations*, also published in 1908, to illustrate the dominant view of Ireland and Irish women within colonial discourse. Ireland was portrayed here in entirely sexualised and gendered terms as feminised and impotent, where 'the virility of the country has been sapped by excessive emigration' and where those remaining were 'stagnating below the line of reason and even sanity'. Despite this degraded state of the country, at least the women knew their place, since 'no country in Christendom reveals a higher standard of chastity' (quoted in Coombes, p. 298). According to the writer, Ireland had the lowest standard of living anywhere in the British empire, and any invitation to marriage for the lower classes (who were group classified as 'solidly Roman Catholic and Nationalist')

would simply mean starting 'another homestead of indescribable dirt
and untidiness, a fresh breeding-place for consumption, the curse of
Ireland'. The representation of Irish women as chaste therefore
stemmed from the British fear of the Irish breeding, which would
lead to further poverty and disease.

The representation of the women in Ballymaclinton was also seen
as a weapon against the more militant aspects of the Gaelic Revival as
represented, for example, by the women of Inghinidhe na hÉireann
and replacing it with 'a "folksy" rendition of what was presented as a
common Celtic heritage' (p. 210). But the colleens 'demonstrating
cottage industries and producing items for sale to the exhibition-goer
in the "village shop", making soap or dancing and singing in their
identical costumes, presented a harmonious picture of archaic and
simple living' (p. 210). Coombes argues that this concept of a
national British culture as a resilient 'folk' culture, surviving in rural
communities of which Ireland was considered one, was a popular
fantasy shared by those at both ends of the political spectrum. She
goes on to claim that this imagery had the clear political purpose of
maintaining the union with Britain:

> Through the living out of a Celtic tradition, eulogised in the
> guidebooks as it was in the press, the 'village' served as irrefutable
> proof of the possibility of a unified Ireland with Protestant and
> Catholic peacefully cohabiting – a harmonious resolution under
> Liberal guidance. (p. 211)

These positive images of the dancing colleens at the exhibition were
intended as a marker of the simple, traditional values that brought
order to everyday rural life in Ireland. This representation of Irish
women as the custodians of hearth and home was not to change
radically within nationalist discourse of the same period, although the
picturesque representations of the dancing colleens at the exhibition
were vehemently opposed by some nationalist women (see Ward,
1983, p. 74).

The colonial racialisation of bodies was also apparent in the
exhibition. The discourse on Irish women's bodies operated by
comparing them with women in other parts of the British empire. It
is worth noting in this regard the stark contrast between the
innocence of the dancing 'colleens' and the threatening sexuality of
the African dancing 'girls'. Coombes (p. 207) observes that the latter
were operating in a context where:

> Physical prowess had already become a naturalised precondition
> of blackness . . . and the concepts of 'natural' racial characteristics,
> biologically determined, is consistent with that emphatic
> preoccupation with the body and with details of black and white
> physiognomy . . .

The popularity of wrestling for black men and dancing for black
women had already been established within this colonial frame. The
sexualisation of the womens' dancing bodies posed a potential
problem for respectable exhibition attendees and the reading public
alike. The problem was solved by keeping the 'perennial' dancers,
but they were now 'described as girls rather than women in order to
play down any hint of unregulated sexuality'. It is interesting to note
that these negative colonial stereotypes of African dance as sexual
display were part of the armoury of the Anti-Jazz Campaign in the
1930s (see Chapter Three). The colonial construction of Irish
women's bodies as chaste, pure and non-violent was set up in
opposition both to Irish men and to African women. These
observations serve to indicate that the 'purity' of Irish women that
later came to be conflated with the 'purity' of Irish dance was not
simply an invention of cultural nationalists but also had roots in the
colonial discourse on Irish women's bodies.

Dance and Irish Cultural Nationalism

Irish nationalist discourse on dance developed in response to the
colonial one. While revivalists wished to refute the negative portrayal
of Irish men as uncouth and uncivilised, at the same time they were
eager to promote the positive representation of Irish women. They
publicly rejected English culture and mores and were keen to
differentiate themselves from them in every way possible. Archbishop
Croke in a letter responding to Michael Cusack's invitation to
become a member of the Gaelic Athletic Association (GAA) gives a
sense of his antipathy towards English products and practices:

> We are daily importing from England not only her manufactured
> goods, which we cannot help doing since she has practically
> strangled our own manufacturing appliances, but together with
> her fashions, her accents, her vicious literature, her music, *her
> dances* [my emphasis] and her manifold mannerisms, her games
> also, and her pastimes, to the utter discredit of our grand national

sports, and to the sore humiliation, I believe of every son and daughter of the old land. (Quoted in Cronin, 1994/5, p. 13)

Croke goes on to accuse Irish people, in what may be an unconscious bid to reverse the position of the Irish as feminised, of slavishly following the 'effeminate follies' of English culture. The GAA provided Croke with the opportunity to counter this effeminacy through developing masculine athleticism in boys and young men through sporting activities. Despite Croke's strong words of criticism, there is ample evidence to suggest that nationalists, while ostensibily distancing themselves from colonial discourse, partially mimicked it.[1] As discussed below, many revivalists were eager to copy the embodied practices that would confer high/er status, either moral or social, and this applied to dance as much as to other embodied practices.

The efforts to shape the dancing body to reflect the body politic led, in my view, to three main objectives: to create a canon that was purely Irish and untainted by foreign influences, to establish and maintain appropriate gender roles in dance and to cultivate the 'civilised' body in dance. How were these objectives to be achieved and who was charged with the task of achieving them?

The Gaelic League and the National Dance Canon

It is widely acknowledged that massive institutional work was invested in making 'culture and polity congruent' (Gellner, 1983, p. 43) by creating distinctive cultural practices in which members of the nation engaged and to which they became attached. In Ireland this work was carried out mainly by the Gaelic League, founded in 1893. The League, as Hutchinson (quoted in Meyer, 2001, p. 68) notes, advocated 'the regeneration of the contemporary nation . . . by a return to its creative source in the evolving Gaelic civilization of its recent past'. Following Garvin (1987, p. 79), Meyer claims that its primary strategy was to return to the values of a romanticised Irish folk culture through the 'preservation and revival of the language, and the celebration of, and if possible the resuscitation of traditional dress, dances, and customs'. While the promotion of Irish dancing was part of its more general aim of folk culture revival, its emphasis in the early days was on language revival and the League's concentration on music and dance was to come later.

However, the cultural politics of dance, especially tensions around desire for tradition on the one hand and the pragmatism of innovation on the other, were clearly present in the first major dance event held by the League in the Bloomsbury Hall, London, on 30 October 1897. The céilí was organised by Fionán Mac Coluim, a clerk in the India Office and Honorary Secretary of the League in London. The location itself serves as a reminder that London was still the cultural centre of pre-independence Ireland and that the choice of venue in the culturally fashionable Bloomsbury area was a sign of the middle-class cultural taste of the organisers. Celtic culture itself had become fashionable among sections of the British establishment at this time as a result of Queen Victoria's championing of Celticism, and of Scottish culture in particular. The 'revival' of the Scottish céilí had proved to be a great success, thereby encouraging the promotion of similar events by Irish cultural revivalists.

We learn from Breathnach's (1983) detailed account that the céilí, though successful, created quite a bit of controversy about the provenance and authenticity of the dances themselves. In dance terms it was an eclectic affair, including, as it did, step dance, music and song, but also sets and waltzes to Irish airs. Solo step dances such as some jigs, reels and hornpipes, because of their intricate footwork and demands on the performer's energy, were beyond the capacity of the ordinary dancer. A compromise was reached with the introduction of new group or figure dances. These involved 'having the men and women face each other in two lines to perform a double jig. When a step had been completed the dancers facing each other exchanged places in a linking movement, so that every other step was performed in the dancer's original position' (p. 49). These dances included the four and eight-hand reels, the *Humours of Bandon* and the *High Caul Cap*. These were less taxing on the performers' energy and were an immediate hit, according to Breathnach. However, it did not prevent many League members from raising objections to their introduction as their provenance was seen to be in quadrilles and, as such, inferior to the native step dances.

The controversy that arose between the 'old and 'new' steps that was a prominent feature of the first League céilí continued to rage from feis to feis and from Oireachtas to Oireachtas and grew increasingly heated and bitter. Opponents became so intemperate that one clerical adjudicator at the Oireachtas denounced the figure dances as a danger to the modesty of Irish maidens and demanded that the Church impose the most extreme penalties on those who practised them. 'Calmer councils prevailed, according to Breathnach (1983, p. 50):

> and the céilí or scoraíocht (both words then misnomers for a night's entertainment of music and dance) became an inseparable adjunct of the language movement. Some of the innate goodness discernible in the step dances thereupon transferred itself to the figure dances and it had been found in their favour that they were the best substitute against the quadrilles and kindred dances. Rincí Gaelacha had arrived and the Gaelic League had saddled itself with an added burden to that of promoting the language.

Cormac Ó Caoimh, the first dance master of the League's first scoil rince (dancing school), confirms the fact that there was an outcry of opposition to these newly composed dances (see Mac Fhionnlaoich, 1973, p. 7). In Meyer's (2001, p. 70) view, the debates 'were so heated that, for a time, the lack of consensus on the issue of national purity in dance almost destroyed the League'.[2]

Selecting dances considered appropriate was an ongoing process. Brennan's (1999, p. 30) analysis of the development of the canon points very clearly to the fact that dance was not just a static reflection of an 'organic' culture but rather was being continuously shaped by the individuals and groups involved in the making of that culture. She describes how Mac Coluim, dissatisfied with the limited repertoire at the first céilí, which contrasted sharply, in his view, with the variety displayed at a Scottish céilithe, found a solution to his problem when:

> fate intervened in the form of an introduction to 'Professor' Patrick D. Reidy, then resident in Hackney, originally from Castleisland, Co. Kerry, who had been a dancing master in west Limerick and Kerry in the late 1880s. Reidy's first classes for Gaelic League members were held in the Bijou Theatre, off the Strand. Here he taught group dances such as the eight-hand reel, the High Caul Cap, and 'a long dance', sometimes termed by Reidy 'the Kerry reel'.

Mac Coluim's party travelled to Ireland to discover more dances and, while they did visit some other places, these trips were confined largely to County Kerry, which was seen to fit the image of the romantic 'Celtic West'. There was also a presumption that Munster was superior in dance terms because of the influence of the dancing masters.[3] According to Brennan, the selection process resulted in the Munster style becoming the national style for Irish dance. The dance collectors were selective not only in their choice of location but also in their choice of dances. Set dances, the most common folk dances in the rural Ireland of the early twentieth century, were rejected on the grounds that they were derived from the quadrilles, which were considered to be foreign, having been introduced into Ireland mainly by the British military. In Tubridy's (1994, p. 27) opinion, even the names of the dances themselves – 'the Lancer', 'the Victoria', 'the Caledonian' – would have aroused suspicion among cultural nationalists. Brennan (1994, p. 23) notes the irony of the Gaelic League position on set dancing in the response to the performance of four-hand and eight-hand reels at the annual conference of the League in 1901:

> Controversy ensued when some observers dismissed the dances as versions of the quadrilles which were classified as alien and thus unsuitable for nationalists. Also excluded as foreign were social dances such as the highland Schottische, the barn dance and the waltz, despite the fact that they were part and parcel of the repertoire of the ordinary people of rural Ireland among whom traditional dance was strongest.

Apart from its foreign provenance, there were other, less frequently acknowledged or articulated, reasons for rejecting set dances as part of the new canon. One of these was linked to social class. Both Hall (1994) and McMahon (2008) attest to the fact that the social-class origins of the prominent members of the League generated an affiliation with 'high culture'. On this basis alone set dancing would have been rejected because of its association with the rural poor and 'low culture'. Hall (p. 94) identifies urban, bourgeois values as predominant in Gaelic Revivalism with the result that:

> interest in so-called traditional styles did not extend to mainstream music-making and dance practice current in rural working communities and that their social dancing . . . was either overlooked or disregarded as being culturally tainted.

League members were equally dismissive. Hall (p. 87) claims, of urban working-class culture:

popular urban music-making and dancing as they existed in the
variety theatres (and much later in the dance halls) were despised
in revivalist circles, partly as they represented cultural impurity,
but, more significantly, as they were expressions of low class vul-
garity . . . In the interests of pursuing the high-brow Euro-British
ballroom dances appeared exclusively on the Gaelic League's ball
programmes.

It is clear from the foregoing that the new dance canon was shaped
by people who had selective and definite ideas about how best to represent the spirit of the Irish nation through the dancing body. It alerts
us to internal tensions in the League, particularly around definitions
of 'traditional' dance and between nationalist and class-based cultural
taste. It also suggests a lack of awareness of their own class biases and
their mimicking of some of the entrenched class ideologies of British
culture. A fine line was being trodden it seems between 'high' and
'low' culture, the new and the old, the traditional and the modern,
the Irish and the foreign, in their negotiation of the canon.

The selective shaping of the new dance canon was buttressed by
the publication of dance manuals used for instructional purposes that
began to appear in the early 1900s. They give unique insights into
the ideal Irish dancing body as, in addition to details of dance steps
and formations, they also specify correct bodily techniques such as
hold, posture and tempo. John Sheehan, a leading member of the
Gaelic League in London and the author of one such popular
manual, *A Guide to Irish Dancing* (1902, p. 48), exhorts his reader:

Don't hug your partner round the waist English fashion. When
swinging hold her hands only. A bow to your partner at the end of
the dance would not be amiss, but be careful to avoid any
straining after 'deportment'. Leave that to the Seoníní. In short
be natural, unaffected, easy – be Irish, and you'll be all right.

This passage reveals a number of dancing rules. Physical proximity
between the sexes is frowned upon, as noted in the advice about
'holding her hands only'. The waist hold is forbidden and regarded
as an English fashion. The dancer must also distinguish himself from
the English by being natural and unaffected rather than straining
after deportment. The author here signals distaste for what he con-
siders to be the mannered, unnatural and affected nature of English
deportment. Sheehan seems to be attempting to counter the negative
Irish stereotype as uncivilised and uncouth on the one hand, but

avoiding the stiff and formal manner of the English on the other. The straining for deportment which he associates with 'seoníní'[4] has clear political overtones, given its reference to John Bull, a symbolic figure of Britishness.

O'Keefe and O'Brien's *A Handbook of Irish Dances* (1902), (see fig. 4) another classic dance manual of the period, also offers instruction about correct comportment including references to posture, tempo and the gender appropriateness of certain steps. In so doing they also inscribe an ideal dancing body. In the following passage they are concerned that dancers achieve an 'ease' and 'grace' of movement:

> There are some features in connection with Irish dancing as it is seen today in Irish towns and cities that call for passing comment. The first thing that strikes any observer is that ease and grace and beauty of movement are almost invariably sacrificed to complexity of steps. When will Irish dancers understand that the simplest steps beautifully danced give more pleasure than the most difficult steps danced with an awkward carriage of the body and with obvious physical distress? It must be patent to anybody who has given the subject a moment's consideration that jigs, reels and hornpipes, danced without grace and ease, become athletic exercises pure and simple, and very often ugly ones at that.

Here we might note the emphasis O'Keefe and O'Brien place on carriage, ease and grace as key components in aesthetically pleasing dance. It is worth observing too the distinction they make between dance and athletics. Although its meaning is not clear to me in this context, it could be speculated that the authors are making a distinction between dance as representational, and therefore capable of symbolising the nation, and dance as athletic, viewed as non-representational or purely technical. The passage continues with further descriptions of the 'perfect step-dancer':

> A perfect step-dancer is not always beating the floor violently, neither is he flying about from one end of a platform to another: his movements are all easy and are performed with a certain stateliness, and the time is clearly but not violently marked. (p. 27)

Could there be a political significance here? There are dangers of over-interpretation but the avoidance of violent moves mentioned twice in the one sentence may imply a rejection of violent or militant nationalism, seen by some as the best way to achieve statehood. And how do we best interpret the authors' concern with dignity, grace, comportment and the balance between uprightness and ease? The upright body in dance does have a wider political significance according to Connerton (1989, p. 90) in his book *How Societies Remember.* He observes that 'much of the choreography of authority is expressed through the body' and that there is an identifiable range of repertoires through which many postural performances become meaningful by registering meaningful inflections of the upright posture. It may well be, therefore, that the dance instructions considered above express a concern with an authority of the body that reflects the political body. O'Keefe and O'Brien's use of the term 'stateliness' is equally interesting. It denotes dignity of carriage when applied to the dancing body but also has obvious political connotations and is a clear illustration of the connection, though not consciously registered by the authors, between the individual body and the body politic. The authors' concern with 'ease' is also intriguing. They lament its absence in dance practice through 'beating the floor violently' (a mark of wildness) and faster than the required tempo (connoting haste and lack of ease). It may mark a desire to be seen as 'civilised' but not stiffly formal like the English, but it may also relate to what Connerton (p. 90) terms a natural postural ease (as opposed to a forced ease) that indicates most accurately the habitual nature of the person and a sense of authenticity.[5] The kind of posture and movement that the authors call for in the dancing body may be seen to correspond to values such as dignity/stateliness, uprightness/honesty, restraint, modesty, ease, grace, authenticity and national pride, called for in the body politic of the Irish nation.

Similar links between the national spirit and appropriate dance movements can be observed in studies of folk dance revivals in Britain at this time. As in the Irish case, it was believed that the revival of 'English country dance' would aid the 'quickening of the national spirit' and would encourage dignified behaviour. Here, too, we see associations between a national spirit, dignified behaviour and a nostalgic longing for English rural values. We also find a similar association between notions of authenticity and correct styles of dance (see Snape, 2009, p. 298). However, because of the different political situations in Ireland and Britain, the mobilisation of national sentiment was of a different order, with different impacts. Snape claims that because England did not experience a prominent nationalist movement in the late nineteenth century it gave rise to a 'moment of Englishness' that was essentially cultural rather than political. In Ireland, however, where there was an ongoing political struggle against British rule, I would suggest that the cultural sphere was marshalled into the service of the political. Consequently, the political symbolism of cultural practices such as dance was heightened.

Reproducing the Nation through Dance

How were these new ideal types of Irish dance to be made popular amongst the people? The League established a system of classes, festivals and competitions on a local, regional and national basis, as other successful cultural organisations such as the GAA and the Catholic Church had done (see McMahon, 2008). Four years after the founding of the League, in the same year as the first céilí, the first feis and Oireachtas were held. Performances of social and competition dancing were organised through a series of feiseanna, aeríochtaí and scoruigheachtaí.[6] The first scoil rince, or dancing school, of the new era had opened in Dublin in 1915. Within a month of starting children's dance classes, fifty had enrolled.

It was by default that the League took on the responsibility for the revival of Irish dance. Initially the League's main concern was the revival of the Irish language as a spoken language of the people and in the early years dance was not high on their cultural agenda. However, leaders within the organisation, most notably Pádraig Pearse, realised that it was necessary to provide popular entertainment such as music, song and dance as well as language instruction if they were to succeed in getting widespread popular support (McMahon, 2008). Meyer (2001, pp. 69–70) also affirms that when it was found that dancing brought in more people than the intellectual debates and political rhetoric, it became an important part of the League's activities. He also suggests that another reason for the League's growing interest in dance was partially their decreasing influence over language after the foundation of the state, when it became involved in language policy development. The League then turned its attention to the dancing programme, which was one of their last intact programmes. It was at this historical juncture, according to Meyer, that dance and politics were becoming increasingly intertwined and the political values placed upon the

spoken language were transferred to dance. Taking on board
Malcolm's (1983, pp. 49–50) observation of the strong links
between the League and Sinn Féin as organisations and that both
'were strongly social and recreational as well as political', he argues
that '[f]or the die-hard revolutionary nationalists Irish dance took on
the rallying role, that had, until then, been played by the Gaelic
Language'. Indeed, he suggests (p. 69) that 'one might well view
dance as the gunpowder of the Irish Revolution' because of the triad
of the cultural as represented by the Gaelic League, the political by
Sinn Féin, and the military in the form of the IRA.

The success of the League in the creation and promotion of céilí
dancing continued. While both céilí and set dance remained popular,
céilí enjoyed a greater prestige in the early years of the century as
they were generally held in well-supervised dancehalls and were supported by people in authority, such as many members of the clergy
and teachers (Tubridy, 1994, p. 26). Meyer (2001, p. 68) attributes
the success of the League to two main factors: firstly, the timing was
right, in that Ireland had lost forty per cent of its population through
emigration as a consequence of the Famine, and, secondly, that the
leadership was unique in its sophistication. Hall (1997, pp. 1–2)
regards its accomplishments during this period as an amazing feat in
that it succeeded in establishing a canon of Irish dance which was to
become the blueprint for future development and practice not only
in Ireland but in the USA, Britain, Australia and in many other places
where Irish people had migrated (see Chapter Six).

Dance, Nation and Gender

It may not seem remarkable that the archetypal dancer addressed in
both Sheehan's and O'Keefe and O'Brien's dance manuals, discussed
earlier, is male. After all, until the 1890s most step dancers were male
and dance instruction would have been historically associated with
the male figure of the dance master. However, the authors O'Keefe
and O'Brien (1912, p. 28) do make reference to female dancers in
terms of the desirability of promoting different dancing styles for
women and men. We learn this from their critique of contemporary
dance practice, which was in their view:

> entirely at variance with the dancing practice of the old dancing
> masters, who always taught women steps of a lighter and simpler

character than those taught to men. This was in harmony with the general good taste of the old dancing master, a man usually of courtly ways and fine manners, ever jealous for the dignity of his profession. To such a man it would have been the source of the most utmost pain to witness a girl 'treble' or 'batter' or perform other manly steps; he possessed a large repertory of light, somewhat dainty steps for women, which were so framed as to make up in grace what they lacked in complexity.

While men were addressed as the lead dancers, the gender composition of step dancers was about to be reversed both in terms of instruction and performance. Evidence from a number of sources indicate that during the period 1890–1920 Irish step dance was becoming increasingly feminised. According to Hall (1994, p. 91–92) competitive dancing which had been an adolescent and male preserve and taught by artisan dance teachers was being taught at the Cork Piper's Club at the end of the nineteenth century to male and female adults, adolescents and children. The latter practice was increasingly adopted by Gaelic League branches during the first decade of the new century. Step dancing, thus 'passed from being a largely adult male rural activity to being one dominated by young urban females'. By the early 1920s Lily Comerford, the first woman to make a career out of dance teaching, had opened a class for children. By the following decade many of the dance classes were taken by young women and the majority of dance teachers were female. Symbolically, too, women were becoming the more ideal figure for representing Irish step dance.

How do we begin to understand this change in the gender dynamics of step dance at the point where it was becoming a key national symbol? On the available evidence it is impossible to provide a definitive answer, but a number of social changes can be noted that may have had an impact on the formation of the female bodies/dance/nation nexus. Women's role in the public sphere was changing and they were beginning to enter some of the professions, most notably primary-school teaching (see Cullinane, 1997). The increase in female teachers of folk dance in Ireland found a parallel in the USA. Tomko's (1996, pp. 171–2) account of the free dance demonstrations of the Girls Branch in the parks of New York city under the direction of Elizabeth Burchenal suggests that it empowered female teachers to gain and claim expertise as folk-dance educators, thereby making inroads into the largely male-dominated enclave of dance pedagogy. Burchenal had travelled Europe, including Ireland, in her endeavour to popularise European folk dances and her philosophies of dance would not have gone unnoticed in her discussion with dance enthusiasts and teachers when she visited Ireland in 1913.

Female figures of the mother (Mother Ireland), old woman/hag (Cailleach Béara) or lover figure (Caitlín Ní Uallacháin) had historically played a key role as symbol of the Irish nation, so it is unsurprising that this symbolic role would be extended to dance. It may well be, however, that there were other dynamics at play and we might look to the context of the changing gender ideologies within nationalism for another explanation of the increasing association of women with step dance. This period was marked by strenuous efforts within cultural nationalism to establish a pronounced demarcation of male and female roles and activities arising from the need for men to reassert their masculinity, which had been diminished under colonial rule (see Meaney, 1993).

Efforts to demarcate gender in the Irish post-colonial context ran in tandem with concerns over gender differentiation in physical cultures elsewhere. Physical cultivation systems, especially sport and dance, were pivotal in marking gender differences. Sport was instrumental, according to Kimmel (1994, p. 33), 'in the fight against the feminisation of men' and 'made boys into men'. The evidence suggests that in Irish culture, too, sport became associated predominantly with men and dance with women. An example is provided by the GAA, an organisation devoted to getting Irishmen involved in manly sporting activities (see Cronin, 1994/5). Alternatively, dance was encouraged for girls because, according to Foley (2001, p. 36), dance reflected 'the belief, until relatively recently, that dance is a girl's preoccupation and too "sissyish" for boys'. For many city girls she believes that Irish step dance became the national physical outlet.[7] Both sport and dance involved the disciplined body and skilled bodily movement but, generally speaking, sport was becoming more associated with men and emphasising manliness and toughness, while dance was becoming more associated with women and emphasising grace and beauty.

Mental as well as physical cultivation systems were also likely to be at play in determining popular ideas about dance. Rationality was

one of the key requirements of political self-governance and an essential feature of modern nation-states. Given the political aspirations of
cultural nationalists, it is likely that the cultivation of rationality was
of primary concern to those seeking to establish an independent Irish
state, and made even more desirable because of the colonial view of
the Irish as irrational. The mind was believed to be the source of
rational thought. The body on the other hand was linked to nature,
the instinctual and the emotional, and deemed to be inferior.[8] As
Thomas observes (2004, p. 191): 'The mind/body dichotomy . . .
constitutes the cornerstone of the western humanist tradition of
thought, wherein the mind is elevated to a spiritual plane and the
body is relegated to the natural, mechanical, instinctual plane.' This
Cartesian model was overlaid on to gender, with men being associated more with the mind and women with the body, including with
dance as an embodied activity (see Ward, 1993). Dominant discourses on dance would have been heavily influenced by the
prevailing gender ideologies and would therefore have been seen as
more appropriate for women.

There were serious gender concerns around dance and other
movement forms in England and the USA at this time. American
men, according to Kimmel (1994), were concerned about cultural
feminisation and the loss of the masculine self. Tomko (1999, p. 4)
also, argues that 'identity formation was at stake in a fundamental
way at the turn of the century' and notes in a brief survey of Chicago
Commons and Boston's South End that folk dancing was deployed
as a female movement practice (see also Snape on the gendering of
English country dance). Ruyter's (1999) study of the Delsartean
movement – a combination of oratory, theatre and physical artistic
expression – is revealing about the role of the body in male and
female performances. The author informs us that most of the men
restricted their performances to verbal recitations whereas twenty-
five per cent of the women also included dance or dance-like pieces,
such as statue posing and pantomime, in their presentations. The
men, on the other hand, used non-verbal expressions as 'enhance-
ment of a text' as opposed to 'an end in itself' (p. 59). Thomas
(2004, p. 190), in her review of Ruyter's book, suggests that men's
preference for engaging with the text rather than with physical
expression in this instance could be attributed to 'the power of the
word' in western rational culture.

If Irish women were becoming increasingly involved in the public sphere through dance activities, and becoming increasingly symbolic-ally associated with national dance, how did this impact on women? Did they regard dance as a way in which they could assert themselves in public? Did they feel empowered by dancing? Or, alternatively, was it a means of controlling them by disciplining their bodies in line with the requirements of a patriarchal national ideal? Were they becoming increasingly the object of the male gaze? Again, without further evidence it is impossible to answer these questions definitively but it may have impacted on women both positively and negatively. It may be useful to draw a parallel once again between the park fêtes in New York and Chicago and the aeríochtaí and feiseanna in Ireland. In both cases young women are engaged with the innovative prac-tice of dancing in public. Tomko's (1996, p. 173) study claims that the park fêtes of the Progressive era performed a dual function in relation to women's entry into the public sphere:

> the salience of the body as a site for inscribing relations of power; and the potency of dance practices for troubling and negotiating meanings. . . . it provided a mode for performing gender – for worrying the circumscription and possibilities for autonomy in the gender role of women that disavowed self-assertion and competition.

Conclusion

This chapter has argued that dancing became a strong marker of national Irish identity towards the end of the nineteenth century and in the early years of the twentieth when Cultural Revivalists sought to bring into being an Irish dancing body that would be appropriate for expressing the spirit of the Irish nation. With hindsight it might appear inevitable that dance would have been singled out as of key symbolic significance to cultural nationalists. However, this chapter has sought to highlight the fact that the shape of Irish dance was not a *fait accompli* from the early days of the Revival but was, rather, continuously struggled over and negotiated during this era. The dis-tinctiveness of the Irish national body was developed, it is suggested, in opposition to the Irish colonial body. It was accidental that dance itself became a primary concern to the Gaelic League and cultural politics operated around the development of the new canon from the early days. Ideas about what was considered to be traditional dance was a source of debate and internal tension within the Gaelic League for many years. Anomalies also existed between the desire by League leaders to revive the folk culture associated with rural Ireland and their orientation towards urban 'high' culture. The ideas of nation and gender were also intertwined in dance discourses of the era that witnessed the symbolic and actual transformation of step dance from adult male to young female. The gender shift requires much more consideration but I have attempted to give a partial explanation in terms of women's increased entry into the public domain giving rise to public anxiety around gender demarcations in cultural practices. From each of these cases it is clear that the dance forms and styles of the new and distinctive canon of céilí dance were influenced by dominant discourses of nation, gender and social class.

Dance was not the only cultural practice to offer a sense of national identity in the early days of the twentieth century. Sport in the form of the GAA could be regarded as equivalent in that both the League and the GAA were cultural organisations in the business of reproducing the nation through leisure activities. The success of the League at this time can be attributed to the fact that they set up their organisation on a local, regional and national level and that a critical mass of people showed great enthusiasm and support for céilí and competition dancing. Dancing of all kinds was a popular and enjoyable activity. By offering a new national canon the League was able to mobilise a people coming out of the traumas of the previous century and looking forward to a new social and political era in the twentieth.

CHAPTER THREE

The Devil in the Dancehall

Church, State and Dance Regulation

The success of the Gaelic League from the 1890s had ensured that 'healthy native entertainments' (Pearse, 1909) were visibly present on the national cultural agenda well into the twentieth century. While the discourse of cultural nationalism revolved around the development of a distinctive Irish culture at the turn of the century, by the mid-1920s it had transmuted into a consolidation of this culture within the newly formed state. It is not surprising, therefore, that dance discourses of the 1920s and 1930s were strongly influenced by issues of concern to the cultural and political leaders of that state. If the pre-state period was characterised by the dominance of the Gaelic League in the promotion of a national dance canon, the 1920s and 1930s were marked by the more prominent role of the Catholic Church and the state in the control and regulation of recreational dance. Their mission was to ensure that the Irish dancing body incorporated the cherished values of the old nation into the body politic of the new state. Since, as we saw in the last chapter, 'traditional' dance was regarded as a valuable cultural legacy from Ireland's past, it was chosen as the most appropriate dance form to represent the future of the nation-state. This chapter addresses two of the main normative and intertwined discourses on dance that emerged during these decades. The first is the binary opposition between Irish and foreign dance, associated with tradition and modernity respectively. Implicated in this double opposition, it is argued, was the issue of gender, specifically the role of women within the national project of the fledgling state and the attendant concern with women's bodies and sexual morality in public discussion of dance. The discourses of dance in these decades reflect the increasing efforts of the state to produce 'docile' bodies (Foucault, 1979).

The polarity between Irish and 'foreign' dance which was apparent from the 1890s was consolidated in these decades against the back-drop of the increasing popularity of commercialised music and dance from Britain and the USA. 'Foreign' dance came to be seen as a contaminant to the purity of Irish culture and, as such, was a source of concern to the cultural and moral arbiters of appropriate movement. It sparked a lively public debate with contributions from a range of clerical, political and cultural opinion leaders including Catholic bishops and priests, members of the Gaelic League and the GAA as well as public representatives at local and national level. Their contributions, widely reported in newspapers of the time, were framed in such a way that traditional dance was perceived as authentic, pure, healthy and graceful while modern popular dances – commonly referred to as 'foreign dances' – were deemed to be inauthentic, impure, unhealthy and dis-graceful. This is a classic case of the 'geographical coding' (Cresswell, 2006, p. 58) of Irish movement as correct and appropriate and the 'foreign' as dangerous and threatening. Intertwined with the geographical, it is suggested, there was a historical coding, since dance became a key site of struggle between the forces of 'tradition' and 'modernity' during these two decades (see O'Connor, 2003).

Jazz dancing was the main object of public opprobrium (see fig. 5). The waltz, foxtrot and quickstep would have been the most common social dances and jazz versions of some dances such as the jazz-foxtrot would also have been in vogue.[1] In reality, the term 'jazz' was somewhat of a misnomer as it seems that all kinds of 'modern' dances came under this umbrella term. Newspaper coverage of the time illustrates the widespread public confusion about its precise meaning. The *Leitrim Observer* of 10 February 1934 in a news article entitled 'What is Jazz?' reports on a discussion of this question by members of Dublin Corporation in which one member, a Mr O'Sullivan, 'caused laughter by asking what jazz was and if some members of the Council would give a demonstration of it for him'. Equally baffled by the term was a member of the Gorey District Committee reported in the *People* newspaper of 17 June 1934 debating a motion whether to support the Gaelic League's call to support their Anti-Jazz Campaign. He expresses his exasperation with the debate so far and with a fellow member of the committee to whom he is addressing his remarks because 'as regards this anti-jazzing business you could not give an explanation of what jazzing is'.

The antipathy towards jazz was based partly on the belief that it was leading to a decline in traditional dance practice. As cultural commentator Terence Brown (1981, p. 41) notes, 'the attractions of the dance hall and the craze for jazz that so disturbed the bishops had done much to put the remnants of Gaelic ways into the shadows'. Confirming Brown and writing in the *Nenagh Guardian* of 29 September 1923, An Fánuidhe Aerach[2] laments the amount of time devoted to jazz in local dance halls:

> 'Jazzing' is the craze of the moment in our dance rooms. We have forsaken the swinging and the 'hop' for the . . . monotony of jazz. The 'Ballycommon' and the Cashel (as it is now usually called) have now become bygones. They are pronounced to be too much of a strain on the physique of our degenerate youth. Three quarters of an hour would cover the time devoted to the truly Gaelic dances, such as the Walls of Limerick, the Waves of Tory, or the Humours of Bandon. It is only the cranks and faddists who take part in them at all. They simply rank as an interval in the continual rounds of jazzing.

Though the author does refer to 'degenerate youth', his critique of jazz is much milder than the unequivocal condemnation by Dr O'Doherty, Bishop of Galway, in his Lenten Pastoral of 1924. Contrasting Irish dance with those imported from the cosmopolitan centres of Europe and the USA, he was of the belief that:

> the dances indulged in were not the clean, healthy, national Irish dances. They were, on the contrary, importations from the vilest dens of London, Paris and New York, direct and unmistakable incitements to evil thought and evil desires. (Quoted in Breathnach, 1983, p. 43)

As well as O'Doherty's explicit reference to foreign dances being a grave offence to moral rectitude, they are by inference unclean and unhealthy.

It is worth making the observation that the 'moral panic' around jazz was not unique to Ireland and there is clear evidence that similar struggles over dance were taking place in Britain, Europe and the USA. Graves and Hodge, for example (1991, p. 119), report on the widespread moral concern that was expressed in Britain about the less restricted style of jazz dance, whose enthusiasts were predominantly young people. They also refer to the fact that at least one local authority refused to let municipal buildings for jazz dancing. A school board in Florida tried to prohibit dancing in 1932 by ruling that any teacher who danced in the school year would lose their job (Adair, 1992).

Notwithstanding the problems with jazz internationally, responses to the problem appear to have been culturally specific. In Ireland the typical solution was to prohibit culturally offensive products and practices, whereas in Britain the norm was to eliminate or transform the degenerate elements but to maintain the overall form or practice. The differences in approach are illustrated in Cresswell's (2006, p. 66) account of the manner in which 'degenerate' foreign influences on English-style ballroom dancing were smoothed out and incorporated into the dance repertoire. The implementation of these changes was effected by the establishment of a regulatory body, the Imperial Society, under the leadership of Victor Silvester, who then became largely responsible for the codification of ballroom dancing. It was primarily the professional dance associations/institutions that became 'the guardians of correct movement' (p. 65). In Ireland, by contrast, it was the combined institutions of the Catholic Church and the state that became involved in dance regulation, with the result that, officially at least, it became legally, as well as morally, binding.

The differences in approach to the problem of 'degenerate' dances in Ireland and Britain must be considered within the wider political and cultural context of the time. In the Ireland of the 1920s there was an increased authoritarianism and conservatism in institutional approaches to culture. Brown (1981, p. 67), for example, claims that:

> a genuinely radical and attractive humanism had fired much of the prerevolutionary enthusiasm for the Irish language and its revival . . . [but] in the early years of the Irish Free State the proponents of Gaelic revival and the supporters of Irish Ireland, in general possessing no real social program, tended to express the need for language revival in terms of conservation and of a despairingly authoritarian control of a society that was becoming increasingly anglicised.

The powerful role of the Catholic Church in the new state must also be taken into account. Not only was it the predominant moral arbiter within Irish society but it also controlled major social institutions such as education and health as well as having its clergy actively involved in cultural organisations such as the GAA. Indeed, many scholars claim that the relationship between the state and the Catholic Church was a confessional one (see Whyte, 1971; O'Dowd, 1987; Inglis, 1998; Ferriter, 2005). The alliance between the Church and state in terms of cultural matters is apparent in the legislation on the censorship of publications in 1929 which banned a number of books and publications that were deemed unsuitable for an Irish readership (see Blanchard, 1953). It was within this climate of authoritarianism that a moral panic developed around popular cultural products and practices from abroad, focused particularly on the changing position of young people and of women in Irish society. The fears and anxieties about these two groups coalesced around leisure activities and in particular leisure activities such as reading, cinema and dancing. This is the cultural backdrop to the concerted efforts documented below to control dance practice in public venues around the country.[3]

Dance, Women and Sin

The term 'degenerate dances' vividly captures the Catholic Church's characterisation of modern/jazz dancing of the 1920s and 1930s. Clerical opposition to dance was nothing new and Breathnach (1983) rightly observes that in both Protestant and Catholic traditions it was a legacy of the puritan attitude of an earlier period. Both the perceived sinfulness of dance and its particular association with female sexuality and reproduction had been established by the sixteenth century, as evidenced in published accounts. The problem for John Northbrooke, writing in 1577, was that 'through this dauncing many maydens have been unmaydened, whereby, I may saye, it is the storehouse and nurserie of bastardie' (p. 37). The rise in the institutional power of the Catholic Church in Ireland in the early to mid-nineteenth century marked an increase in the control of priests over the behaviour of members of their parish. One Dr Murray, Archbishop of Dublin, ordered that the parish priest 'deliver in writing' to him accounts of 'Public Abuses' including 'Public Dances' before his visit to a particular parish (quoted in Inglis, 1987, p. 154). The women/dance/sin nexus was established very early on in public discourse, with women's bodies being marked as a source of temptation and even as inherently unclean. Alexander Irwin, writing in 1836 on instructions for priests hearing confessions, urged that:

if the penitent be a girl, she should be asked whether she has
adorned herself in order to please the men? Whether for this
purpose she has used paint, or stript her arms, shoulders or neck?
Whether she has spoken, or read, or sung anything immodest?
Whether she is not attached to somebody with a more peculiar
affection? Whether she has not allowed herself to be kissed.

Dances were singled out for attention by the archbishops of
Ireland in a pastoral address in 1875 that warned about the dangers
to purity and modesty inherent in theatrical shows:

> we must add the improper dances which have been imported into
> our country from abroad, to the incalculable detriment of morality
> and decency. Such dances have always been condemned by the
> Fathers of the Church. This condemnation we here renew; and we
> call upon all to whom God has entrusted the care of our immortal
> souls, to use every exertion to banish from our midst what is
> clearly of itself an occasion of sin. (quoted in Breathnach, p. 43)

The waltz, which was to become one of the most popular social
dances, was met with moral outrage on the part of the Catholic
Church because it was believed to flout the virtues of modesty and
chastity that had become essential for women. The following editorial in the *Catholic Penny Magazine* states the Catholic position:

> Is it not possible that a Christian company cannot exercise them-
> selves, or take a few hours of agreeable relaxation without having
> their shoulder bare, or their bosoms uncovered? Do they ever
> think upon the tremendous consequences of their subjecting
> themselves or others to gross temptations? But it is not merely the
> dress, but the manner of females, that we condemn. Can a lady of
> the least virtue, or modesty, behold, much less take part in some
> of these scandalous dances, called Waltzes, in which common
> decency is set at defiance? . . . Every lady then, of virtue, and of
> decency, who wishes to preserve her character pure should utterly
> discountenance such an invasion on the pleasures of private and
> public life. (quoted in Inglis, 1987, p. 201)

The long tradition of the interlinking of dance, women and sin in
the pre-Famine Church in Ireland was strengthened further in the
post-Famine period. Writers agree that there was a much more liberal
attitude to heterosexual relations/reproduction accompanied by high
marriage rates in pre-Famine times. Where the staple diet of the
majority of the population was potatoes, the land could be subdivided

and the potato crop from a small plot was sufficient to sustain a number of families. The failure of the potato crop in successive years, culminating in what has come to be known as the Great Famine of 1847, led to total devastation of the social fabric with starvation, disease and emigration and an estimated reduction in population from eight to four million people. This kind of trauma had widespread and long-term consequences for those who survived and remained in Ireland. Those who owned or leased land were no longer willing to subdivide. Instead, a system of primogeniture was put in place whereby the eldest son inherited the land and his siblings were forced to find a livelihood elsewhere, either through emigration or, as frequently in the case of second sons, as Catholic priests. Consequently, the institutional Catholic Church that grew in power in the post-Famine period and its clergy, being largely comprised of farmers' sons, were acutely aware of the need to regulate sexual reproduction.

The exclusive focus on sexuality as the predominant morality in post-Famine Ireland led to an excessive concern with women's bodies. In this regard Inglis (1998) observes that:

> Women especially were made to feel ashamed of their bodies. They were interrogated about their sexual feelings, desires and activities in the confessional. Outside the confessional there was a deafening silence. Sex became the most abhorrent sin. (p. 199)

To ensure that occasions of sin were avoided, physical contact between the sexes had to be restricted. And because dancing presented just such an opportunity for contact it is hardly surprising that it was to become one of the main activities to be policed by the Church in post-Famine Ireland.

Degenerate Dancehalls

The legacy of the Church's attitude to dance outlined above was very much in evidence in its public statements on dance during the 1920s and 1930s. These most commonly took the form of pastoral letters composed by the bishops in which the dancehall was singled out as a 'degenerate' space and a source of moral danger and corruption. In 1923, the Archbishop of Dublin warned that:

> Dancing had become a grave danger to the morals of their young people, not only in the city but in the country parts of the diocese

and parents were warned that God would demand a strict account
of them if, by their want of vigilance, they allowed their children
to be led astray from the path of virtue. It was a matter of noto-
riety that the dances often were of a kind imported from other
countries and were, if not absolutely improper, on the border of
Christian modesty. (quoted in Breathnach, p. 43)

In 1925 the Bishops issued another major statement on the evils
of dancing, with express instructions that it be read quarterly in
churches across the country. Dancehalls were blamed for the increase
in alcoholism, unmarried mothers and the wave of infanticide which
one judge described as being so common that it had become 'a
national industry' (quoted in *The Irish Times*, 2 March 1929). The
dancehall exercised the guardians of public sexual morality greatly
and became the primary site for the close monitoring of women's
appearance, demeanour and conduct. In a joint pastoral of the Irish
hierarchy issued in 1927 the purity of the Irish race is seen to be
under threat from the devil's work in multifarious guises:

> The evil one is forever setting snares for unwary feet. At the
> moment his traps for the innocent are chiefly the dance hall, the
> bad book, the indecent paper, the motion picture, the immodest
> fashion in female dress – all of which tend to destroy the virtues
> characteristic of our race. (quoted in Whyte, 1971, p. 27)

The Jesuit priest, Fr Devane,[4] himself the author of a number of
writings on illegitimacy and on dance outlines the danger dancehalls
posed to women's virtue. Supporting his case in an article in the *Irish
Independent* of 7 September 1929 he writes:

> Havana, the capital of Cuba is virtually danceless, following orders
> issued by the Department of the Interior for the closing of all
> dancing halls and academies, as a result of charges of immorality
> brought against them, says a Reuters message. The Government
> has received hundreds of protests against these dancing places
> from women's clubs and religious organisations, which branded
> them as 'dens of iniquity' and 'pitfalls for young womanhood'.

For Devane (1931, p. 170) the dancehall was both 'a moral and
national menace' and his strongly held view was influenced by a
report to the County Homes Committee in which the
Superintendent Assistant Officer's information, based on his visits to
various districts of the county, led him to the view that:

there could be no doubt that the dancehalls all over the county were a great source of evil to girls. In some parishes there were as many as three or four such halls. Some of these halls, he had been informed, were run by private individuals for the sake of profit, as they charged an entrance for all who attended, and were quite indifferent as to the character of the individuals who went there . . . There can be no doubt that certain depraved persons went from a distance in motor cars for sinister purposes. (p. 177)

We might note here Devane's objection to the commercialisation of dancehalls but it is less a critique of the commodity form as such and more a lament that dance was moving out of the control of its moral guardians. The disinhibiting effects of alcohol were equally problematic for him: 'Not only is drink taken by the men but girls are induced to do so. Hence the orgies one sees so often reported in the Press and which centre around the dancehalls' (p. 171).

Women, Dance and Public Space

Public pronouncements on dance and dancehalls formed part of a wider debate on public sexual morality that was in turn sparked by the perceived sharp increase in public immorality and illegitimacy rates in the period since the foundation of the state in 1922. It would be unfair to lay all the blame for the women–dance–sin nexus on the Catholic Church. In fact, the belief that dancehalls were both a dangerous and degenerate space for women was much more widespread. Opinion leaders in the GAA, the Gaelic League, local and national politicians, and the national press all expressed concern about the state of public morality. Women's vulnerability was of particular concern and illustrated most clearly in the setting-up of the Carrigan Committee by the government of the day to report on widespread prostitution and on the physical and sexual abuse of young women. Though the Committee presented the report to government in 1931 it was never published because the findings 'starkly contradicted the prevailing language of national identity formation with its emphasis on Catholicism, moral purity and rural ideals' (Smith, 2004, p. 216).

The Irish Times took up the topic of immorality and vice in the editorial, 'Irish Morals', on 2 March 1929. Breathnach (1983, p. 45) makes the point that, while the newspaper could not have been regarded as a mouth-piece of the Catholic hierarchy, it was 'every bit as fierce as the bishops in lamenting the situation'. Summarising the main points of the editorial he noted that:

> It repeated the claim for Ireland's high reputation over the cen-
> turies for the cardinal virtues of social life, for the chivalry of its
> men and the modesty of its women, but it went on to say that
> reports of trials and statements of judges suggested that in many
> parts of the 26 counties, especially in the south and west, standards
> of sexual morality had become lamentably low. The abominable
> crime of rape was frequent; infanticide, one judge declared, had
> become a national industry! The growing immorality was not the
> outcome of revolt against hardship in the home. It sprang from
> sheer defiance of all convention, from a complete lack of principle.
> Whatever the cause, it had assumed the proportions of a national
> problem. The clergy, judges and police were all in agreement con-
> cerning the baneful effect of drink and low dancehalls. Further
> restriction on the sale of drink, strict supervision of dance halls, the
> banning of all-night dances would abolish many inducements to
> sexual vice, but what was needed above all was recognition of the
> fact that the nation's proudest and most precious heritage was slip-
> ping from its grasp.

It is clear from the extracts above from both clerical and secular sources that dance discourses were part of a more general 'moral panic' (Cohen, 2002) about immorality and vice, youth in general, inadequate parenting and the corrupting influence of 'foreign' enter-tainments. As we have seen, women's bodies became the locus of these more generalised anxieties and in particular the appearance, demeanour and behaviour of these bodies in public. This concentra-tion of interest indicates a degree of ambivalence towards, and fear of, women in the public sphere. Gray and Ryan (1997, p. 522) testify to such ambivalence when they identify a tension in the symbolic rep-resentation of womanhood as virgin/whore in the early years of the Irish state. In their view:

> The bad woman was not merely responsible for her own moral
> downfall and for the ruin of men but threatened the moral degen-
> eration of the entire nation. Immoral literature, indecent dress
> and modern dances were all largely responsible for lowering the
> standards of Irish womanhood.

McAvoy (1999) supports the assertion that women were to blame for sexual non-conformity at this time. They were represented, she suggests, as at one and the same time childlike, vulnerable and easily seduced, but also as having moral responsibility for men's proper conduct and thereby presenting the greatest danger to moral probity and sexual purity. The call to Irish mothers by Cardinal O'Donnell in 1926 for the chaperoning of young women illustrates the latter's perceived innocence in the face of men's predatory nature. O'Donnell urges mothers 'to provide the close attendance of a capable female companion, and not leave them altogether unshepherded in the lonely ways where the wolf may prowl in seeming innocence' (quoted in Breathnach, 1983, p. 44).

Dance scholars confirm that ambivalence towards women dancing in public is common (e.g., see Bordo, 1993, p. 5). Cowan (1990), in her ethnographic study of dance in rural Greece, claims that this type of ambivalence is noticeably present in a society where there is uncertainty about, or antipathy towards, women in the public sphere. Ireland of the 1930s was just such a society. Throughout the decade women were either nudged out or in some cases forced out of the public sphere and obliged to retreat into the private/domestic space (see O'Dowd, 1987).[5] So while, on the one hand, women's bodies were seen as extremely vulnerable, on the other they were feared as presenting a threat to a distinctly patriarchal order.

Punishment of errant women was advocated by some clergy. Breathnach (p. 43) cites the same Bishop O'Doherty of Galway who, having referred to six cases publicly known since the last confirmation of girls having fallen, advocated stern parental control as follows:

> Fathers of this parish, if your girls do not obey you, if they are not in at the hour appointed, lay the lash upon their backs. That was the good old system and that should be the system today.

The oft-quoted bishop merits another mention in the *Leitrim Observer* of 17 February 1934 entitled '"Giddy Girls" Warned':

> 'We cannot' says the Bishop of Galway Most Rev. Dr O'Doherty 'close our eyes to the fact that the evil of impurity is on the increase. Want of parental control, evil reading, senseless company keeping and above all, degenerate dance halls, are the chief causes of corruption. There are impure men who would willingly prey upon innocence and inexperience. But there are also some giddy girls who by the levity of their words and actions are often more guilty than their partners in crime. There was once a public

penance for public crimes of impurity: I hope that it may not be necessary to reintroduce it.'

Two elements in the extract above are worthy of note. The first is the manner in which the attribution of blame is being shifted from men onto women, and the threat of punitive action if warnings went unheeded. The second is that the admonishment is limited to 'degenerate dance halls' and, by inference, to modern/jazz dancing and to the category of 'modern' women.

Because modern women were widely believed to be a threat in public spaces, their presence there had to be strictly monitored. Women appearing in public were to preserve modesty at all costs. This included dance but pertained to appearance and physical movement generally. The following newspaper extract from the *Leitrim Observer* of 19 May 1934 gives a sense of the ways in which women's public appearance and activities were perceived to be problematic. It is a report obviously culled from another provincial newspaper of a discussion at a Wexford County Council meeting regarding regulations with respect to public decency. One of the suggestions voiced at the meeting was for the introduction of a bye-law so that '*persons* [my emphasis] in bathing costumes be prohibited from promenading public roads and other places other than the immediate shore unless wearing wraps or overcoats'. One of the contributors from the Wexford County Board, Mr T. Cooney, responded that 'We are not supposed to be critics of *ladies*' [my emphasis] bathing dresses'. Gender in this instance is not initially attributed but is subsequently inferred. There had been no mention of gender in the interchange until the last statement and, though the speaker is adopting a liberal stance on the issue, the interchange itself serves to indicate a distinct nervousness about women's bodies in public space.

A more extreme antipathy towards women displaying themselves in public or mingling with members of the opposite sex is captured in an extract from the *Wexford People* of 10 February of the same year – in this instance, on the sports field. Dr J.C. McQuaid, who was later to become Archbishop of Dublin and was at the time president of Blackrock College, a prestigious Catholic school for boys, was protesting against what he termed the 'un-Catholic and un-Irish decision' taken at the annual congress of a national athletics organisation in favour of women competing in the same athletic meetings as men. 'I hereby assure you', he is quoted as saying, 'that no boy from my college will take part in any athletic meeting controlled by your organisation at which women will compete no matter what attire they may adopt'.

As with dance, antipathy towards the 'modern woman' was not confined to the Catholic clergy but formed part of a wider culture of complaint. The following newspaper report of a woman's death at the remarkable age of one hundred and twenty-three was used as an opportunity, as the subheading indicates, to be a 'Critic of the Modern Girl'. The woman in question was reported in the *Leitrim Observer* of 24 February, 1934 as saying:

> Her [the modern girl] dress is nothing but a ridicule . . . It would make a modest man blush. The cosmetics she uses make me ashamed of being a woman at all. Her late hours and *dance hall amusements* [my emphasis] will not help her reach my age.

While some warnings to women were based on national incidents and events, other snippets, originally culled from overseas newspapers and probably copied from the Irish national press, were also included. Under the heading of 'Lipstick Banned', one such short item reports that 'An order forbidding Catholic women to use lipstick during the Eucharistic Congress has been given at Buenos Aires' (*Leitrim Observer*, 20 October).

Whether from local, national or international sources, the message to the 'modern woman' was unequivocally normative (see also Ryan, 1998) and pointed to the dancehall as a potentially dangerous and degenerate space.

Dance, Rurality and Mobility

The references above to 'dens of iniquity' located in cosmopolitan centres such as London, Paris, New York and Havana might lead one to presume that the problem lay in the occasions of sin presented by urban living. However, it was rural dancehalls that were singled out for the strongest criticism. *The Irish Times* editorial quoted earlier opined that, while Dublin's crime and vice were associated by many reformers with the wretched housing conditions of the slums, 'it appears that an even more formidable laxity of morals prevails now in rural districts where that excuse is not valid'. And it is the 'baneful effects of drink and low dancehalls upon rural morals' that is of particular concern. Fr Devane believed that the problem was due to the relative lack of surveillance and supervision in rural areas:

> The more isolated is the district, the greater the danger. In the larger towns, which are well-lighted and where the dancers move, as a rule, from the dance to the home along the lighted streets, there is not so much harm done. But in lonely country places the dangers are too obvious to need description. If the dance were confined to the people of the district one could be more tolerant. But, when it is open to all and sundry who come from many miles away, and who are complete strangers, then a new element of danger becomes only too apparent.

The lack of adequate supervision in rural halls is also mentioned by Bishop Morrisroe in the diocese of Achonry in the Lenten Pastoral in 1929:

> There is one agency, which Satan has set up here and there in recent years, that does incalculably more harm than all the others we have mentioned. It deserves to be called after his name, for he seems to preside at some of the dark rites enacted there. We have in mind the rural dancehall, owned by a private individual . . . conducted with no sort of responsible supervision, a cause of ruin to many innocent girls . . . One need not have a lively imagination to realise the possibilities arising from promiscuous mingling of the sexes under conditions so favourable for the machinations of wily corrupters from far and near, who swoop down on their innocent prey with the greedy rapacity of Harpies.

The concerns about the vulnerability of women and the rapaciousness of men was associated in particular with rural dancehalls because of their relative isolation and difficulties of monitoring behaviour in and around them. It also applied to dance platforms. A 1939 report (Department of Justice file No.8/21) by J.J. Cooney to the Limerick Superintendent regarding dancing in Kilcornan parish reported the following:

> There are two cases of unmarried girls in this locality becoming mothers. In one case the trouble is due to company keeping during or after the dances at this place. In the other case the dance platform is indirectly the cause as the couple commenced keeping company at dances here last summer with unhappy results.

Increased mobility facilitated by new modes of transport, particularly the motor car, were seen to increase anonymity and hence opportunity for escape from the local area. Traditional methods of control in small rural communities were based on personal knowledge of each member so that parents and other figures of authority such as the clergy could keep an eye on young peoples' company-keeping. Increased geographic mobility was seen as a threat by the bishops and singled out for mention by Cardinal McRory in his Pastoral Letter of 1931:

> Even the present travelling facilities make a difference. By bicycle, motor car and bus, boys and girls can now travel great distances to dances, with the result that the quietest country parish may now be attended by unsuitables from a distance. (quoted in Smyth, 1993, p. 51)

These 'unsuitables from a distance', akin to Simmel's (1908) idea of 'the stranger', are ever-present figures of danger in these discussions. The classic story of the 'Devil in the Dance Hall' illustrates this point well: the young girl is dancing with the 'tall dark stranger' and is about to accept his offer of seeing her home, when she looks down to the dance floor and notices his cloven hoof!

The clergy's attitude to rural dance may also have been influenced by an ambivalence towards rural life. This may have had its source, as with Gaelic League activists discussed in Chapter Two, in the tension between views of the 'folk' as 'authentic' and 'salt of the earth' on the one hand, but as uncouth and ignorant on the other. Negative attitudes towards country people, who were regarded as close to nature and the animal world, had prompted 'civilising' attempts from the nineteenth century on. Cardinal Cullen's 'Romanising' policy from the 1850s amounted, in Hall's opinion (1994, p. 35), to an 'attack by the church on rural social behaviour – directed against violence, drunkenness and sexual immorality which were associated with dancing at patterns and fairs'. The increase in these behaviours since the foundation of the state gave further credence to the public belief that rural life was in dire need of moral reform.

The Catholic Church would also have perceived a threat to their power in other individuals' or groups' ability to mobilise communal activities and to facilitate engagement with alternative ideas and lifestyles. This could include dancehall and cinema owners as well as other rural intellectuals who circulated ideas and reading matter, some of which might have been antithetical to the Church's teaching. Jim Gralton was such a person. A socialist and returned emigrant, he built and ran a dancehall – the Pearse–Connolly Hall – in Gowel in 1922 but, in doing so, 'he posed an institutional challenge to the church's determination to secure its position as the sole focal point for communal organisation in the locality' (Gibbons, 1996, p. 100). Because of his socialist ideas and activities he drew the disapproval of the local clergy and was eventually forced to close the dance hall and leave the area.

Foreign Bodies and the Anti-Jazz Campaign

As noted above, critiques of the dance halls were inextricably intertwined with those of jazz dancing and in combination they provided a common enemy to be defeated if the moral integrity of the country was to be upheld. The debates and struggles around jazz and dance regulation which had begun in the 1920s continued for at least a decade, at times abating and at others becoming more heated. The Anti-Jazz movement regained strength in the 1930s and the Gaelic League relaunched its Anti-Jazz Campaign in 1934. County Leitrim was the location for the most vociferous opposition to jazz in the figure of Fr Peter Conefrey, parish priest of Cloone, who believed that jazz was both a smokescreen for international communism and a flagrant display of sexuality. Writing in the *Catholic Pictorial* in 1926 he asserts that:

> Jazz is an African word meaning the activity in public of something which St Paul said 'Let it not be so much as named among you'. The dance and music with its abominable rhythm was borrowed from Central Africa by a gang of wealthy Bolshevists in the USA to strike at Church civilisation throughout the world. (quoted in Gibbons, 1996, p. 101).

While Conefrey's views on jazz, particularly its imputed connections with international communism, may initially appear bizarre, a similar fear of Bolshevism emerged at this time in the ballroom dance circle in Britain. Speaking as organiser of a meeting of ballroom dance instructors at the Grafton Galleries in London in 1920, Richardson warns of the dangers of increased liberalism on the dance floor:

> Unfortunately just as in the big world the struggle of liberty had on occasions gone to extremes and in places developed into

bolshevism, so in the ballroom there has been a tendency towards
an artistic bolshevism. (quoted in Cresswell, 2006, p. 60)

This extract reminds us that, while some dance discourses in Ireland
were culturally specific as I have argued, others formed part of a
wider international circuit of dominant ideologies about the social,
political and cultural issues of the day.

Conefrey's objections to the overt sexuality of jazz dance point to
the association of ideas about sexuality, race and dance, which coa-
lesce into an overtly racist attitude. Its association with black/African
sexuality was regarded as both primitive and threatening (see Back,
1997). Jazz was also believed to have a deleterious effect on rural
youth. Though published eight years after the passing of the Dance
Halls Act, the GAA publication *National Action: A Plan for the
National Recovery of Ireland*, written under the pen name Josephus
Anelius (1943, p. 112), laments the fact that:

> In most rural districts there is no social meeting place for young
> people, except the idle crossroads by day and the jazz hall by night.
> The demoralizing influences of this condition do not appear to be
> fully recognised by parents and other responsible people.

Newspapers carried numerous reports of resolutions adopted
against jazz dancing by county councillors and of protests against the
broadcasting of jazz music on national radio. The *Leitrim Observer* of
3 March, 1934 reports on a meeting held in Manorhamilton to form
a branch of the Gaelic League:

> Mr Brian Gilgunn said there was a society called the GAA which
> would expel members for attending foreign games and at the
> same time its members were the greatest exponents of jazz
> dancing. If it was wrong to attend foreign games, it was much
> more wrong to attend jazz dances.

If the extract above is an accurate reflection of the reality, it indicates that the official normative approach to jazz in cultural
organisations such as the GAA did not go uncontested and at least
some members ignored it. This evidence of contrary opinions and
practices within the GAA is a timely reminder that actual dancing
behaviour cannot simply be read off from the normative discourses of
the moral crusaders whose views were widely reported in the
newspapers.

The Anti-Jazz Campaign was not entirely about the prohibition of jazz dancing, however defined, but also included objections to all-night dancing and a demand for legislation to restrict dancing hours. This dual concern can be detected in the following extract from Cardinal McRory. Speaking from a position of self-acknowledged ignorance of jazz dance he nevertheless condemns it wholeheartedly:

> I heartily wish success to the County Leitrim executive of the Gaelic League in its campaign against all-night jazz dancing. I know nothing about jazz dancing except that I understand that they are suggestive and demoralizing: but jazz apart, all night dances are objectionable on many grounds and in country districts and small towns are a fruitful source of scandal and ruin, spiritual and temporal. To how many innocent young girls have they not been an occasion of irreparable disgrace and lifelong sorrow? (quoted in Smyth, 1993, p. 54)

The public pressure on government from organisations supporting the Anti-Jazz Campaign mounted. Finally bowing to this pressure the government introduced the Dance Halls Act of 1935 that legislated 'to make provision for the licensing, control and supervision of places used for public dancing, and to make provision for other matters connected with the matters aforesaid' (1936). The main section of the Act banned the holding of unlicensed dances and a fine could be imposed on those without a licence. Licences could only be granted by District Court judges, who set conditions on the days, time, venues and personnel to whom licences could be issued. In considering applications, the judge was to take into account 'the character and the financial and other circumstances of the applicant for such license' (Dance Halls Act, p. 10). The introduction of the Act signalled at least a pyrrhic victory for those involved in the campaign. But what did the Act achieve and how did it affect public dancing?

Extant accounts provide somewhat fragmented and, at times, contradictory evidence about the effects of the Act. There were obviously some initial problems with unintended consequences and the blanket ban on privately held dances affected private clubs, crossroads dancing and 'at homes'. A letter from Donnchadh Ó Briain, TD, claimed that the Act was: 'never intended to cover Crossroad Dancing which is a survival of a time-honoured source of amusement and social intercourse free from any of the abuses associated with the modern Dance Halls' (Department of Justice file No 8/21).

A case was also reported in which local Gardaí threatened to institute proceedings against the organisers of Irish dance classes held in
a non-licensed hall in Ballymurry, County Roscommon. A hand-
written internal Department of Justice memo dated 22 February
1940 indicates that 'The Minister is sympathetic to the case made by
the promoters, he is anxious that the Irish dance, part of our cultural
revival, should be encouraged'. There are also newspaper accounts of
people who were prosecuted for holding private house dances.
However, it is difficult to interpret the fact that the number of pros-
ecutions following the introduction of the Act in 1936 were
relatively few and it begs the question as to whether people were
extremely law-abiding or whether, alternatively, the legislation was
not rigorously implemented across the country.

The Dance Halls Act is frequently blamed for the demise of house
dances in those parts of the country where they were still extant.
With reference to County Clare, for instance, where house/set
dancing had been an integral part of local life, there are a number of
accounts that support this position (Breathnach, 1983; O'Connor,
1991; Ó hAllmhuráin, 2005). For instance, Gearóid Ó hAllmhuráin
(p. 17) claims that 'the transition from the country house to the
village hall, facilitated by the Dance Hall Act, dislodged music and
dancing from the familial to the public domain'. And the compelling
arguments they make are frequently based on the first-hand accounts
of dancers. Tubridy (1994), however, sees other factors coming into
play in the demise of set dancing. (See Chapter Five, and also Austin
(1993), on the Dance Halls Act).

There is a danger, however, in depending exclusively on the published accounts of moral prohibition of jazz of extrapolating to the
actual behaviour of the dancing population. In other words, there is
a bias in favour of the belief that people abided by the rules of the law
and the moral crusaders. Whatever about the former, the latter
seemed to be greeted with mixed reactions. My aunt (born in 1910)
would have been dancing around this time in County Wexford and
she thought the prohibitions were largely ignored: 'In the beginning
there was a whole uproar about waltzing . . . the tight embrace . . .
[it was] cried-down by people in authority, then they had to get used
to it because the people waltzed in spite of them.' It is probable that
reactions were mixed, that some sections of the population resisted
clerical demands, that others totally ignored them and that some

were partially bound by their constraints. More detailed research would be needed to establish which groups and social classes were likely to respond in particular ways.[6]

The regulation of dates and duration of dances covered by the Act may have resulted in affecting daily routines and time-frames. The ostensible reason given by campaigners for objecting to all-night dances was that they were a moral danger to young people. However, this element of the legislation – a normative specifying of hours devoted to leisure – may also be seen as a way of introducing urban/industrial time-frames, schedules and production values into Irish rural life. This is borne out in the reference to both the rational and economic benefits of dance legislation in a letter written by Justice Louis J. Walsh, Justice of the District Court in Letterkenny, County Donegal, to the Department of Justice on the draft bill: 'My colleague and myself in this county are endeavouring to restrict dancing to *reasonable* [my emphasis] hours, – the orgy of all-night dancing which was taking place was both a moral and an *economic* [my emphasis] evil.'

It is also well to bear in mind that some of the reasons for state intervention in the regulation of public dancing had nothing to do with moral welfare but with health and safety issues such as over-crowding and inadequate ventilation in dancehalls, issues that were becoming increasingly centralised as the responsibility of government.

The Dance Halls Act was also seen to play a symbolic role in cultural relations between nationalist and unionist traditions in the North of Ireland. *The Bell*, the leading critical journal on Irish cultural and political affairs of the time, opined that the legislation had created a wedge between Protestants in the North of Ireland and the Free State by confirming their perception of the Free State as sectarian:

> When a Northern Protestant complained that he had previously enjoyed an Irish jig, but now, as soon as a fox-trot was heard, the Gaelic Leaguers immediately withdrew in protest, the result was that Protestants in their turn refused to dance to traditional Gaelic tunes. (Quoted in Goldring, 1993, p. 158)

While the efforts of Church and state in regulating dance in the 1920s and 1930s were ostensibly devoted to promoting the traditional and eschewing the modern, it could be argued that in some respects they had the opposite effect. The Dance Halls Act enabled the state to benefit in a number of ways from recreational dance. Firstly, it facilitated the control of leisure, disciplining bodies in line with urban/industrial time-frames. Dance changed from a largely non-profit-making activity into a commercial one (see Chapter Four for more details). The profit from dances that had hitherto gone to families in need or local community projects was now going to individual dancehall owners. The state too began to make a profit from dances in the form of an annual entertainment tax that was introduced in 1932 and continued intermittently until 1962.[7] Recreational dance was thus being promoted as a business enterprise in which the state both controlled and gained from it. It seems ironic then that the antipathy towards modernity expressed in the Anti-Jazz Campaign should have unwittingly been instrumental in encouraging forms of governance that were more centralised, more rational and more bureaucratic – in effect more modern.

This chapter has addressed the way in which the normative discourses on dance in the 1920s and 1930s was influenced by the key concerns of the cultural and moral arbiters of the relatively new state. I have argued that these decades were characterised by a climate of economic protectionism and cultural authoritarianism in which a binary opposition between Irish/traditional and foreign/modern culture was overlaid on to a moral discourse in which Irish/traditional was designated as good and the foreign/modern as evil. Furthermore, I have suggested that political, church and cultural leaders in responding to the social and cultural changes in Irish society created a moral panic about 'modernity' in general and about young people and the 'modern' woman in particular. The widespread fear of losing control over the behaviour of these groups led them to attempt to control their leisure activities and in particular popular and modern cultural activities such as dance. However, their attempts to keep Irish dance from contamination by the foreign were generally ineffectual. The appeal of modern music and dance was far greater for the majority of the population than that of traditional dance and, despite warnings from on high, dancers literally voted with their feet and flocked to the ballrooms that were playing modern music and were beginning to spring up all over the country. This is the subject of the following chapter.

CHAPTER FOUR

Ballrooms of Romance
Dance, Modernity and Consumption

Recreational dancing was one of the most common leisure activities for young people in Ireland throughout the 1930s,'40s and '50s, with ballroom dancing being the predominant dancehall repertory. It is the romantic discourse that developed around ballroom dancing in these decades that is the focus of this chapter. The dancehalls themselves, it is argued, were constructed as romantic utopian spaces in which dancers could play out their identities. Furthermore, I make a case for the role of dance in ushering in new forms of identities for women in particular; identities that aspired towards and aligned themselves with the urban and the modern, and with an ethos of romance and consumption. If, as discussed in the last chapter, the 'modern' woman was represented as a potential threat to social order in the 'degenerate' dancehall space in the 1920s and 1930s, I want to propose that by the 1940s this image was being challenged and she had been transformed into a romantic and glamorous figure to be both envied and emulated on the dance floor.

In pursuing the theme of this chapter I draw on a number of sources. It opens with a discussion of the establishment of public dancehalls in the 1930s and innovations in dancing that were effected in the original 'Ballroom of Romance' in Glenfarne, County Leitrim (see fig. 6). The chapter then goes on to examine how the links between dance, romance and consumption have been theorised, with specific reference to women, followed by evidence of how these elements are constructed within the dancehall space. The discussion then moves on to women's personal reminiscences of the pleasures of dancing in the 1940s and 1950s. Finally attention is drawn to the tensions and contradictions in the 'romantic utopia' of the dancehall.

Public Dancing and Ballrooms of Romance

Despite the campaign against 'modern' forms of music and dance discussed in Chapter Three, available evidence clearly suggests that the vast majority of Irish people preferred to listen and dance to 'modern' music. Indeed, Brown (1981, p. 41) as indicated in the previous chapter claimed that these modern influences were apparent very soon after the Treaty was signed in 1922 and the 1920s saw the increasing domination of the American–British ballroom repertory in dancing in Ireland.[1] A number of dance venues were established to cater for the increase in the popularity of public dancing as a leisure activity. In addition to the building of parish halls a number of privately owned/commercial dancehalls were built (see fig. 7). The building of halls proliferated in the 1930s, in part because of the demise of house dancing as well as the increasing popularity of 'modern' dance music and the emulation of musical and dance trends from abroad, especially Britain and the USA.[2] While there are no reliable sources of information on the exact number of dance venues in Ireland at this time,[3] we do know that the opening of ballrooms continued into the 1940s, when the renowned National Ballroom opened in Dublin in 1945 and the equally popular Seapoint opened in Salthill, Galway, in 1949. The increase in dancehalls during these decades was not confined to the cities but was also evident in larger and smaller towns and villages. However, the dance halls to which I refer in this chapter, the bigger, more luxurious venues, were generally, though not exclusively, located in cities and provincial towns.

I am proposing that these dance venues fostered the performance of romance in everyday life and drawing on Eva Illouz's (1997, p. 120) claim that '[r]omance is lived on the symbolic mode of ritual, but it also displays the properties of the staged dramas of everyday life'. She notes how 'the use of artifacts (clothes, music, light and food), the use of self-contained units of space and time' are used to produce these staged dramas. Applied to the Irish context, dancehalls could be seen as one of the primary self-contained units of space in which artefacts such as décor, music, lighting combined to create a romantic ambience and were important props in the unfolding of the staged dramas of everyday life.[4]

An account of the reputedly original 'Ballroom of Romance', opened in Glenfarne, County Leitrim, in 1934 and recorded in a radio interview with the owner, John McGivern (RTÉ, 1985), helps to give some sense of the innovations in the dancing space that were intended to foster romance and that were to become commonplace over the next two decades. Having emigrated to the USA in 1930 at the age of seventeen, McGivern returned four years later to fulfil his ambition of building and running a dancehall originally called *The Rainbow*. The 'Ballroom of Romance' was added later as an addendum to the name, as it was the first public dancehall in the west of Ireland to explicitly promote romance as part of the evening's entertainment. Incorporating as it did McGivern's ideas for a new type of dance venue and influenced by his experience of dancehalls in the USA, the evening's programme included spectacle, gimmickry and showmanship. McGivern adopted a stage name, Johnny Macaroni, borrowed from a radio presenter in the USA. He advertised the dance in five provincial newspapers including those in the adjacent counties of Donegal and Sligo. Connecting the face with the product, he included a photograph of himself in the advert on the advice of the editor of the *Sligo Champion*, who reminded him, rather tellingly, 'you're in the entertainment business' and advised that the more publicity he could get the better. He wore a dress suit for the opening night, signalling the special quality of the occasion and the venue. As master of ceremonies, it appears that McGivern presented himself as both a character in, and director of, the 'staged drama' of the ballroom.

Romance was the main theme of the 'staged drama', since McGivern's expressed objective was to encourage the (respectable) mingling of the sexes in the ballroom. Coming from the local area himself, he was familiar with the lack of interaction between men and women, the shyness of men[5] and the scarcity of women (McGivern, 1985). In order to break down the familiar segregation of the sexes, in which men congregated on one side of the hall and women on the other, he introduced the 'Romantic Interlude'. This was initiated by the men inviting the women to dance and if they failed to do so they were asked to leave the hall! Dancers were then asked to shake hands, kiss and make a date with their partner. McGivern hoped that getting everybody to get to know each other through dancing would in time lead to courtship, marriage and the reproduction of another generation. It is unclear how successful his tactics proved to be in the local catchment area. What we do know is that at a national level all efforts to stem the tide of emigration were ineffective since a steady stream of emigration continued throughout the 1930s and 1940s, with the highest number, half a million people, leaving in the 1950s.

The radio interview with McGivern gives a valuable insight into the mutual accommodation between local cultural entrepreneurs like himself and the local clergy. Unlike the dancehall owner Jim Gralton (mentioned in Chapter Three), who was forced to close his dancehall because of clerical interference, McGivern overcame the clergy's initial objections to his hall.[6] His account serves to highlight the fact that in some respects dancehalls posed a dilemma for the clergy in so far as dancing, while potentially an occasion of sin, was also the venue for meeting marriage partners, who would in turn produce a new generation and thereby ensure the survival of the local communities on which the clergy depended for their livelihood. This was coupled with a concern for parishioners' spiritual welfare in the sense that there were fewer perceived dangers (even allowing for the many enumerated in Chapter Three) to moral welfare at home than abroad. From this perspective it would not have been in the clergy's interest to oppose all dancehalls and in these circumstances their chief concern was to ensure that the dances that were held were 'properly' conducted. McGivern illustrates how he succeeded in winning over the clergy in an anecdote about a visiting Redemptorist priest during a mission in the area. On learning that he had been criticised from the altar, McGivern invited the priest to the dancehall to see for himself how it was managed. The priest accepted and when he witnessed how well run the dances were, he changed his mind and went on to praise McGivern's enterprise with the words, 'I wish there were more people in Ireland like you'. For his part, McGivern skilfully melded the rules of decency and respectability with those of romance by lowering the lights for the Romantic Interlude, but, as he assured the radio listener, 'never too dim'. At the end of the evening, and borrowing again from the US radio presenter, McGivern confirmed the Christian ethos of his establishment with his parting words to the dancers: 'Good night, good luck and God bless you all!'

The importance of transport to dances was another issue raised by McGivern. It took a while, he recalled, for the hall to get off the ground, as its success was dependent on people coming from outside the area and travelling relatively long distances to the dances. The opening of *The Rainbow* coincided with the gradual increase in the ownership of bicycles and cars, which facilitated greater geographical mobility and with it the opportunity to travel to dances outside the local area (see Smyth, 1993). This gave young people an opportunity to meet new people, thus lending a heightened sense of novelty, excitement and anticipation to social interaction. These 'strangers', classified in the clerical discourse as 'unsuitables from a distance' and the source of ruin for young girls, now became easily transformed into the romantic male figure of the 'tall dark stranger'.

Women, Romance and Consumption

Discourses of romance and consumption are inextricably linked. According to Illouz (1997, p. 65), '[a]s participation in the leisure markets became increasingly associated with romance', she claims, 'the experience of romance became increasingly associated with consumption'. Her observation that '[t]he incorporation of romance into the marketplace' was achieved through a process of commodification could equally be applied in the Irish context and to recreational dancing in particular. The increase in leisure goods and services from the 1930s is illustrated in the construction of the commercial dancehalls already referred to as well as in the increase in car ownership and cinema attendance. However, it is important to bear in mind that actual consumption was unevenly distributed both geographically and in terms of social class, and that the majority of the population were relatively poor. The national political and economic situation of the time would have put further constraints on actual consumption, since the economic climate of the 1930s was characterised by a state policy of protectionism and an economic war with Britain that restricted the availability of consumer goods and encouraged the value of frugality. However limited actual consumption practices may have been for the majority, what was important was the creation of an aspirational consumer culture through popular media such as film and advertising.[7]

Discourses of consumption and romance are inextricably linked to discourses of gender. There has been a long historical association between gender and consumption, with women being one of the first groups to be targeted as consumers. Veblen (1953 [1899]), one of the earliest writers on the subject and who coined the term 'conspicuous consumption', was the first to acknowledge the particular role of women in the consumption process. In households of married couples, he suggests, 'the system of honorific expenditure and conspicuous leisure by which this good name is chiefly sustained is therefore the woman's sphere'. Women had become a target market from the late nineteenth century via channels such as women's magazines, which advertised products and services both for themselves personally and for the bourgeois household for which they had the responsibility of management. The establishment of large city department stores in the late nineteenth century provided women with a comfortable space in which to consume. The advent of radio soap opera in the 1930s provides yet another example of the interlinking of women, consumption and popular leisure.[8] Women remained the main target market for consumption until other markets, and particularly the youth market, were identified in the era of 'mass' consumption after the Second World War.

Coupled with the consumption ethos was the growth of the ideology of femininity, with an emphasis on the presentation of women *qua* women and the desire for goods that enhanced the appearance of femininity such as clothes, jewellery and cosmetics. I have argued elsewhere (O'Connor, 2005) that the display advertisements for female fashion and beauty products in the provincial press from the 1930s reflected the cultural cachet, service ethos and modernity of the metropolis.[9] Analysis of these advertisements revealed that the content, mode of address and juxtaposition of advertisements combined to construct the reader as an embodied individual female consumer. However, it would be misleading to suggest that it was only women who were targeted as consumers. Men were also, but in a different way and with different products. Advertisements aimed at men were for utilitarian products associated with work such as boots, animal welfare products, farm implements and machinery. Where they were targeted at men's leisure activities, it was generally for items such as tobacco, not, as in the case of women's products, purporting to enhance their appearance or transform their sense of self. In many cases the illustrations for ladies' fashion and beauty products were placed next to advertisements for leisure activities such as dances and cinema, their juxtaposition being yet another illustration of the intersecting worlds of the cinema and the dancehall (O'Connor, 2005). In this way the advertisements set up a dichotomy between the local and the cosmopolitan, creating a sense of fantasy around the extra-local which paralleled in many ways the other more glamorous and exciting world of cinema.[10] These observations are supported by the literature on the ideology of romance which attests to the fact that it is directed towards women through popular fiction, film and women's magazines.[11]

The symbolic power of the association between dance and cinema, referred to above, was further enhanced in some cases by the physical proximity of the spaces of the dancehall and the cinema. Sometimes they shared the same building, as for instance in 'The Mars' cinema/ballroom in Kilrush, County Clare, which was used for dancing when the seats were taken out. The Town Hall in Loughrea, County Galway, was a two-storey building, the bottom floor used as a cinema and the top floor as a dancehall. In the latter they also shared staff, with the usher in the cinema also working as the buffer of the dance floor. Films themselves, it could be claimed, were the purveyors *par excellence* of the romantic imagination. A significant number of the narratives of Hollywood films shown in cinemas around the country were stories of romance (see Byrne, 1997). As well as this the diegesis of some films linked dance specifically with romance, particularly 1930s' musicals starring Fred Astaire and Ginger Rogers (see Kuhn, 2002, for discussion in the British context) and, in the 1950s, with Doris Day, Gene Kelly, Anne Miller and Lesley Carron. Romantic and dance films or films which included dance were generally very popular with women. The influence female stars had on dress and hairstyles as well as on behaviour such as smoking has also been widely observed (see for example Byrne, 1997; Stacey, 1994; Kuhn, 2001). Terence Brown (1981, p. 186) believes that these cinematic images were partly responsible for large numbers of young women emigrating from rural Ireland in the 1940s because they believed they could have a better life elsewhere:

> The lure of the urban world glimpsed in film and magazine, made emigration less awesome, gave a sense of possibility to what in the past would have been experienced only as the workings of implacable fate.

The Dance-hall as a Utopian Space

'To me it was just wonderland.' 'It was utter glamour . . . the music was out of this world.' These comments from dancers at Seapoint

(1999) and the National Ballroom (2002) respectively illustrate the fact that dancehalls gave dancers the opportunity to transcend their everyday reality and enter an alternative, more exciting and magical world. Dancehalls were instrumental in creating what I call a 'utopian space'. I am drawing here on Dyer's (1992, p. 18) use of the term with reference to the experience of popular entertainment in which he sees utopia as a sensibility rather than a political model. As such he is more concerned with 'what utopia would feel like rather than how it would be organised'. The particular aspect of Dyer's analysis which is pertinent to the discussion here is that popular entertainment tries to fulfil certain needs, one of which is that for abundance in a world of scarcity and inequitable distribution of material resources. And one of the ways in which entertainment provides for this need is by creating a 'sensuous material reality' (p. 20) that consumers enjoy. In the dance context, the 'sensuous material reality' is created through association of the dancehall space with glamour and abundance. This effect is achieved partially through what in film terms would be called the *mise-en-scène* – elements such as music, lighting, décor, quality of the dance floor, as well as the dancers' appearance and demeanour – the latter being all-important in the creation of the spectacle of dancing couples moving across the floor.

The names of the dance venues themselves signified glamour and romance; names such as *The Savoy, The Gaiety* and *The Pavilion* evoked an urban theatrical and cinematic ambience with connotations of luxury and cosmopolitan sophistication. Some names, such as *The Waldorf,* located as it was in the small village of Woodford, County Galway, may have stretched imaginations to their limits. In terms of décor, some, such as *The National* in Dublin's Parnell Square, were fitted with wall mirrors, a crystal ball rotating from the ceiling and velvet-covered seats, all helping to create an atmosphere of luxury and romance. In addition, the full-length wall mirrors, in which dancers could see their own reflection and the reflection of the other dancing couples, enabled a kaleidoscope of gazes, inviting comparison with other couples and hence invoking both the admiration and envy of other dancers.

The bands playing these venues – some even had a resident orchestra – conveyed an aura of glamour. Formally dressed in dark suits or uniforms and sporting bow ties, these men, as one dancer observed, were 'like film stars'. One of the reasons Cathleen gave for liking the big bands was because:

> there'd be three rows of musicians, there'd be the drummer and trombone and a trumpet . . . saxophone and clarinet, and a fellow playing the piano and all that and they be dressed up in a uniform, red jacket and grey trousers with braid . . .

The musical programme structured the mood of the evening and the main dances would have been comprised of the old-time and slow waltz, quickstep and foxtrot. The pace slowed towards the end of the evening and the last dance was generally a slow waltz danced to a romantic musical number such as *Good Night Sweetheart*. For women to be invited for the last dance usually meant that their partner would offer to see them home, perhaps leading to a first date. As Cathleen recalls, 'the last dance was something special . . . the guys kind of asked their favourite girls for the last dance . . . it was a kind of signal that you were regarded as *a special person* [my emphasis] if you were asked for the last dance'.

'Urlár sleabhan, go hiontach i gcomhar damsha!' (A slippy floor, great for dancing!) was the comment of a regular dancer in Seapoint. The quality of the floor was seen to be important for dancing and maple was considered the best wood for the purpose. The floor needed to be properly and regularly maintained so as to ensure the correct amount of traction: enough polish to allow the dancers to move in a seemingly effortless way around the floor but not too much so that they could maintain their balance.

Lighting was also a major prop in creating a utopian space as it could be used effectively to create an aura of magic and romance. Lighting has frequently been an effective technique in creating a dream world of consumption, starting with the early department stores where 'women were held spellbound by the motionless elegantly clothed models poised under electric lights' (Williams, 1991, p. 221) and where electric lights succeeded in 'elevating ordinary merchandise to the level of the marvelous' (p. 218). It is likely that the effect of electric lighting in dancehalls would be heightened by the fact that it was a novelty in many areas until the 1950s, when the ESB's Rural Electrification Scheme provided the service country-wide. As in a stage set, the lights could be dimmed or brightened according to the mood one wished to create. The rotating crystal ball became a regular feature of many halls, creating yet another magical lighting effect, bathing the dancing couples in soft, dappled light. The later addition of spotlights created a similar effect and gave rise to competitions with 'spot prizes' – small, but relatively luxurious items such as a box of chocolates or a pair of nylon stockings. The use of the spotlight was a common technique in the process of creating 'stars'. Equally, its effect in pinpointing dancing couples gave them the feeling of being 'special' and might be regarded as prefiguring the transforming of other ordinary people into 'stars' in contemporary reality TV talent shows.

In addition to cinema, other media such as newspapers would have played a key role in constructing the dancehall as a glamorous, modern space through reports on dances and through advertisements for upcoming dances (see O'Connor, 2005; and fig. 8). The following example from the *Connaught Tribune* of 16 June 1934 illustrates the rhetoric involved including allusions to high levels of personal attention, comfort and convenience offered to dancers:

> The season at the Dance Pavilion, Salthill, Galway is now in full swing. With an excellent maple floor and a good band the Pavilion provides *everything possible for the enjoyment of dancers* [my emphasis].

In a similar vein, an advertisement for a dance at the *Gaiety*, Carrick-on-Shannon, claims that '[t]the hall possesses all facilities which go to make it one of the best for dances being well lighted, modernly equipped and heated, and having a specially-sprung floor for dancing' (*Leitrim Observer*, 3 November, 1934). In this piece dancers are addressed as individual and modern consumers whose comfort and enjoyment are ostensibly of concern to the proprietors, who purport to offer the best facilities as well as the most up-to-date music and dance schedules. Other advertisements for the *Gaiety* strive to reinforce its reputation as the dance venue *par excellence*. The 'Grand Opening Dance' announces that Charlie Harvey's Capitolian Band will be providing the music and:

> Visitors to Dublin who heard this band at the Capitol Theatre will appreciate the quality of the music engaged for the occasion. They will present a programme containing all the *new* [my emphasis] orchestral selections and the *very latest dance* [my emphasis] hits . . . It is hardly necessary to say that this is one of the best halls in the West for dancing, *possessing all the necessary*

essentials for comfort and convenience [my emphasis]. The catering will be under the *personal* [my emphasis] supervision of the Management, and as on former occasions the details as to the wants of patrons will be exactingly looked after. (*Leitrim Observer*, 22 September, 1934)

An account of a Ballina Post Office Dance held in the *Arcadia* ballroom reported that it:

proved to be a huge social success. 'The loveliest and most per-fectly arranged function of its kind held in Ballina for years' was the general opinion of patrons . . . The decoration of the hall evoked general admiration. The scheme was carried out by . . . and his work certainly left nothing to be desired . . . The recherché supper supplied at Moylett's café, was splendidly served and much enjoyed. (*Wexford People*, 17 February, 1934)

In this way, dance advertisements and reports of dances in the newspapers operated by constructing the dancer as modern, offering novelty in the form of the latest facilities and the most professional dance bands from outside the local area. I suggest that this type of advertising and reporting would have had particular appeal to women, purporting as they did to offer glamour, luxury, romance as well as cultural capital (note the use of the French word *recherché*) to the dancing experience.

It is well to bear in mind that the attractiveness and glamour of these dance venues derived partially from their contrast to the rela-tively more spartan environment of the local dance venues. The rhetoric of glamour and novelty noted in the above extracts appear in advertisements for bigger halls in the larger urban areas, which sug-gests that these were the halls that could boast of the superior facilities advertised. Conversely, the smaller rural halls did not, or could not, boast of such modern facilities (cf. figs. 8 and 9). In this way the opposition between the discourses of tradition and moder-nity are overlaid on the distinctions between rural and urban.

Staged Dramas in the Romantic Utopia

The dancehall, as we have seen above, was the stage on which dancers could perform the 'staged dramas' (Illouz, 1997) of the romantic utopia. It is to the performance of the drama that I now turn as expressed in conversations with dancers themselves. Though there is a gap of approximately fifteen years between the newspaper representations above and the oral accounts of dancing presented below, similar themes emerge: themes that link consumption, romance and modernity to the experience of dancing.

With increasing urbanisation and the resulting geographical mobility, Ireland of the 1950s was becoming a society in which identities were gradually changing from ascribed to achieved. Ascribed identities which had up to now been the norm, especially in small-scale rural communities where everyone knew everyone else and individuals could easily be 'placed' according to their kin, began to decline. There was a corresponding increase in achieved identities particularly in urban environments, where anonymity was the norm. In such an environment, the 'presentation of self' (Goffman, 1959) and especially the creation of first impressions through appearance was becoming increasingly important as a marker of individual identity. The leisure space of the dancehall was the primary, and in some cases only, venue that offered the opportunity for displaying the adorned individualised female body because in the work environment there was generally a requirement for uniformity of appearance. Appearance was of primary concern to the women to whom I spoke and they reported investing a considerable amount of time, effort and income in their personal appearance. Dressing-up/fashion, cars, meals, drinks and tickets were recurring topics of conversation.

Dressing up for dances was both a duty and a pleasure.[12] In one dancer's words, 'it was very much the thing to wear the right clothes particularly going dancing'. Other dancers confirm the importance of the 'right clothes':

> The protocol again would be ballroom dancing, then the big event of the year would be Lalor's of Naas ... had a Milk Producers' Dance every year ... ballroom dress ... you wouldn't dream of going without your long dress. (Betty)

But women also dressed up for ordinary dances as well:

> You'd dress up for the ordinary hops in a summer dress or something ... they had these things called stiff slips at the time to make your dress stand out and you know we used to have layers of these on under the dress and then there was another fashion of felt skirts, circular effect, stiff slips underneath them ... they

rustled as you danced, swung out and everything . . . the boys used to love them . . . you know they really did love the skirts when they'd swirl they'd twirl you around. (Cathleen)

That iconic item of clothing, fashionable in the 1950s, the multi-layered underslip, or the 'stiff slip', was mentioned by many of the women to whom I spoke. Made from several layers of gauze, it was similar in style and effect to the ballet dancer's tutu, emphasising the femininity of the wearer. It could be seen as an important prop in the 'staged drama' on the dance floor as it very effectively framed the body of the individual female dancer and made a rustling sound as the dancer moved. It had the effect of making women feel both special and feminine as well as creating an aura of abundance and luxury.

While the women emphasised the importance of dressing up for dances, it is also clear that their disposable income was limited. However, they succeeded in making the most of their limited resources, what de Certeau (1984) refers to as 'making do':

> You'd wear them every day but you wouldn't wear all these slips under them, you know going to work you'd just wear the summer dress and an ordinary slip under it . . . long gloves and you had to have a stole. (Betty)

Referring to dress dances, Cathleen observed:

> You really had to dress up for this (dress dance) you had to have a long evening dress and they [partner] wore the bow tie like they do now . . . I was very fortunate, my two sisters both got married in the one year, both married in 1956 and I was bridesmaid to both of them and I organised a dress that I could wear afterwards to dances, to dress dances . . . I had a little bolero over one of them so that it was completely strapless and I just wore a bolero over it in the church.

Clothing styles were influenced by Hollywood film stars, as we see in the following extract:

> [We] tried to dress like Doris Day, little white collars, narrow velvet ribbons around the neck. White nylon blouses were fashionable with white pearl buttons, or in pale pink, pale mauve, pale yellow . . . and the dirndl skirt with the underslips which you starched and hung on the line.

In this quote it is worth noting the pale 'feminine' colours and styles that were fashionable amongst Hollywood stars during the 1950s and which the women imitated.

The 'Cinderella effect', the transformative capacity of clothes, is also apparent in Kay's comments on the dress she wore in a group photograph of couples at a dinner dance: 'I bought that dress in the Munster Arcade in Cork . . . twenty-nine (pounds) was a fortune at the time. I thought I was beautiful.' We might also note the high proportion of her income that she spent on the dress. Breda referred to the magical effect created by a dancer's dress when she was still too young to be allowed to go to dances:

> When it came to the time of a dress dance, what we call 'the Dance' those famous dances . . . there was a big shop on the corner and we'd watch them and we'd admire them and they'd all come in in their long dresses . . . and they'd all come in their different colours . . . satin . . . no . . . taffeta . . . it made a nice rustle and we'd watch them there and wonder who were they going with . . . it looked like something out of this world . . . fairyland. (Breda)

In the extract above we can see the repetition of references to materials such as tafetta, satin and velvet, all of which create 'sensuous materiality' and which was also a feature of other elements of the dancehall space. For all of these women the items of clothing and accessories made them appear special and transported them to another world of romance, glamour and sophistication. Crucially, it also highlights how the dancers performed their gender identity, in this case of hyper-femininity, by presenting themselves in the fashionable and ultra-feminine styles of the time (see figs 10, 11 and 12). One woman reflecting on her dancing days in the 1950s saw it as a 'very nice fashion time, very feminine'. It is also the case that the women's repeated references to the objects of desire associated with dancing serve to corroborate Illouz's claim of the inextricable links between romance and consumption, and, in this case, the further link with dance.

Romance is generated not only through the structure of the dances themselves, but also at the level of sensate experience and more specifically the pleasurable feelings of gliding, as one is led by one's partner across the dance floor. It is no coincidence that the phrase 'being swept off one's feet' connotes the double sense of falling in love and of dancing. Cathleen recalls with regret the demise of couple dancing because of the type of dance hold and physical connection with her partner that it afforded:

> I think when the rock and roll started I think it was the end of the era of the foxtrots and that because when we went to dances first the men held you in their arms . . . but then the rock and roll started . . . throwing you out . . . and then within no time they were into the disco . . . beside one another and danced.

Kay commented too on the pleasure of being led in the dance:

> and they would get you up and they would lead you around the floor, the more masterful they were, the more you enjoyed it. They knew what they were doing and they looked back and could see there was a space to dance. I enjoyed that better than anything really.

There appear to be at least two aspects of pleasure associated with being led on the dance floor. One is the desire to be held in someone's arms, as expressed by Cathleen. This desire to be cared for on the dance floor echoes to a degree the rhetoric of the newspaper advertisements for dances quoted earlier in the chapter, where personal attention and being cared for is offered by the dancehall proprietors. Kay's comments emphasise more the 'masterful' aspect of men's lead role in the dance. While nuanced differently, both comments demonstrate the way in which the closed-couple dancing of ballroom serves to reproduce traditional gender roles and provides a good example of 'gender performativity' (Butler, 1993) on the dance floor[13] (see fig. 12).

The moving in unison with a partner also appears to generate what Kuhn (2001) refers to as the sensate experience of 'heterotopia', a concept initially coined by Foucault and meaning the possibility of occupying contradictory spaces simultaneously. She found that the appeal of 1930s musical films especially those starring Fred Astaire and Ginger Rogers motivated the respondents in her study to dance all the way home having seen the cheek-to-cheek number in the film *Top Hat*. Kuhn suggests that the filmgoers-cum-dancers were imbued with feelings of power in their gliding movement across the floor from a mundane reality into a 'space of their own' and that the two spaces become one.[14] It was the merging of the ordinary and extraordinary spaces that was an integral part of their enjoyment.

Contradictions of the Romantic Utopia

While the recollections of the 1950s dances are by and large nostalgic memories of a happy youthful time, they were also redolent with tensions in the romantic utopia. The ritual of preparing for dances was in many cases an all-female subculture of camaraderie and fun that might usefully be seen in Goffman's (1959) terms of a backstage region where they gathered before the performance. Betty, who worked and lived with a group of other young women recalled the preparations with palpable pleasure:

> the getting ready was as enjoyable as the night itself and it would start . . . there would be thirty of us girls, and I think only two bathrooms, and you start to get ready around seven [pm], it would be an ongoing thing, and the fun of it was . . . a crowd of girls and we used to run in to see what the other had and borrowing from each other, 'twas great . . . you could say like that, it was half the enjoyment of it.

Differentiation between a frontstage and backstage region is also present in comments made about relaxing after the dance. The women were conscious of the fact that glamour had its price and Cathleen spoke of the damage to her feet from the shoes she wore to dances – 'the high-heeled shoes were crippling' – and claims that her friends who went dancing with her now have similar trouble with their feet. To relieve their feet on the way home from dances they used to put the shoes in the basket of the bicycle and pedal home in bare feet.

Women's choice of dance partner was limited, since it was generally a man's prerogative to invite women to dance and generally unacceptable to refuse. Referring to *The National*, one woman recalled that 'girls couldn't dance with girls and if you refused to dance with a man you could be told to sit down for the rest of the night'.

Women's enjoyment of the dance was sometimes marred by clumsy partners, as Cathleen acknowledged in the following:

> I remember one guy saying that to me one night, he asked me to dance and he kept standing on my toes, he said to me, 'You'll just have to excuse me, I've just washed my feet before I came out, and I can't do a thing with them! [laughs] Those days women said that about their hair' . . . well I suppose you just went along with him [partner] and tried to teach him . . . if he admitted that

he couldn't dance . . . you'd be fed up particularly if the good
tunes that you loved [were being played], this guy was falling all
over the place.

Some women tried to ensure that their partners were good dancers,
especially if attendance at the dance entailed spending a lot of their
hard-earned money. There is a sense of exchange, of a *quid pro quo*,
in the following extract:

Well, usually when we'd go to the dress dances we'd go with a
partner, [you] could go on your own [but] if you didn't have a
partner you just wouldn't go . . . to a dinner or dress dance you'd
have to have a partner. You'd know your partner's capabilities
before you went, whether he could dance or not, it was always
one of the big items, you wouldn't go with him if he couldn't
dance . . . it did come into it, it did with me anyways because if
you buy a nice dress and all that goes with it, it always worked out
expensive if you had to buy a long dress and all that goes with it,
well if you go to one of these, you want to make sure your partner
can dance before you go there. (Kay)

Women saw the necessity of being popular, as nobody wanted to
be a 'wallflower'. As one woman observed:

It was more the dancing that we liked than looking for a fella, to
get up for every dance, you'd come home and say, 'I really
enjoyed that', marvellous that you weren't left sitting for any
dance, you know you'd be up the whole night . . .

The extract above suggests that 'looking for a fella' wasn't a primary
motivation for going to dances. However, despite the earlier reference to female camaraderie, the conversations also revealed an
element of competition amongst women with regard to their ability
to attract men, conveyed in the following extract:

Yes you would always have one of those . . . the envy of every girl
in the hall [laughs] and especially if she got the best-looking man
in the hall . . . mostly those type of girls were very unpopular . . .
they would know that they were good-looking or the best
dressed . . . you might get the odd one who wouldn't, but the
majority . . . inclined to be self-centred, we always thought that,
we'd say 'look at her, doesn't she think she's the bee's knees' and
you'd take an instant dislike to her . . . you'd get one in your own

group who'd think that she could do anything she liked or get any man in the hall. (Betty)

The women were also aware of the tensions between the romantic and moral discourses that necessitated the negotiation of the rules of behaviour on the dance floor. The following conversation with Cathleen on 'close dancing' illustrates the point:

> C: Talking about close dancing, that was the big thing, you weren't supposed to be dancing close to the boy you know . . . used to say to you 'it's a sin to dance too close to a boy'.
>
> B: What did you think?
>
> C: I went along with it . . . if a guy was holding you too tight, you'd push him away a bit . . . say he fancied you and be dancing with his cheek up against your cheek . . . that wouldn't be allowed. In some places, I never saw it in Dublin, but I believe they used to have somebody around the dancehall telling them to move back a bit you know, or they wouldn't let them dance cheek-to-cheek, but I used to dance cheek-to-cheek a lot . . .
>
> B: How bothered were people by what the priest said?
>
> C: Oh, they were, you know. We'd go to these missions . . . in the church . . . and the women would go the first week and the men would go the second week . . . and the women would go and there'd be murder from the pulpit . . . dancing close and all that sort of thing, jigging around too much at dances you know, shaking yourself too much, your body would be kind of gyrating or something . . . make it very arousing for the men you know.
>
> B: And how did you deal with that kind of thing?
>
> C: It never worried me.

Here we can observe how personal behaviour is differentiated from what is perceived as a more general response to the Church's teaching on 'close dancing'. There is also a differentiation between what Cathleen regards as appropriate: cheek-to-cheek dancing was acceptable whereas too tight a body hold merited some censure. In this context it is interesting to note that my aunt, who was of an older generation (and quoted in Chapter Three in relation to the decrying of the waltz by the local clergy), went on to mention that '[I] liked the waltz . . . well, the way it was you know, you had to be a good girl, hadn't I?' The switching of the pronoun from the third to the first person appears to express her internalisation of society's norms but also a tension between moral probity on the one hand and the pleasure of the dance on the other.

There was also an etiquette surrounding acceptable partners at dress dances.

> If you went to dress dances with a boy, there might be a party of you . . . then they'd all ask you up to dance within your party. But if there was a guy at another table and he looked over and he would fancy a girl at another table, there would be no way that he would come from his table across and ask her to dance, he could only ask within his own party . . . it was frowned upon, the girl that he would have asked would be looked upon as being a fast kind of a girl, had thrown her eye over to him or something. (Cathleen)

Here it is the woman who was labelled as 'fast', whereas it was the man who had initiated the action. In most instances women were dependent on men for transport home. As Breda remarked, 'another reason you were interested in getting a fella was to go home because the dance didn't end until four or five o'clock and you had to have somebody'.

From the comments above we can see a clear expression of ambivalence about some aspects of the staged performances on the dance floor and the dance event in general. There was explicit complaint about commonplace physical discomforts in attempting to achieve a feminine look. There was also a more diffuse awareness of greater imbalances in gender power and the ultimate realisation that their own lay substantially in their attractiveness to men. So while at one level the dancehall was an escape from everyday reality, a place of fantasy and pleasure, at another it was a place in which they had to present themselves in the best possible light to maximise their chances of finding a suitable husband.

Conclusion

In this chapter I have suggested that a distinct link between ballroom dance, romance and consumption was forged in Irish dancehalls from the 1930s to the 1950s. The growth of ballrooms during this period created what I have referred to as a 'utopian space' – a space of romantic possibility – for dancers through both the ambience of the dancehall space itself, produced through elements such as music, lighting and decoration, location and through the staged romantic dramas that were performed there. Furthermore, these spaces both reflected and assisted in generating an ideology of romance that was gendered in a number of significant ways.

Performances of gender were pivotal in the staged dramas of the dance floor: a heightened sense of femininity was generated through dressing-up and through the predominance of couple dancing as well as in the female camaraderie in the preparation for dances. Women's recollections of dancing confirmed the importance of dance in their lives and the pleasures of going dancing. While the dancers' accounts of their experiences confirmed the existence of the 'romantic utopia', they were simultaneously aware of its contradictions in terms of the imbalance of power between men and women. The establishment of the commercial dancehall as a venue and of ballroom as the most dominant form of social dancing can be linked to the social changes that were taking place in Irish society at this time and by concomitant changes in cultural identities. Traditionally marriage in rural Ireland was regarded as an economic alliance of farm families, and arranged marriages were common. While the evidence suggests that there may have been elements of personal attraction and liking between the marriage partners prior to marriage, this was variable at best, and was certainly not the primary consideration in the alliance. At a time when traditional matchmaking was in decline, the dancehall became the primary space in which young people met their future marriage partners. It thus became associated with courtship practices. Dancing therefore both reflected and enabled an emerging discourse of romance where individual attraction, rather than family alliances, became a more important consideration in choosing a marriage partner. In symbolic terms the closed-couple dancing of ballroom represented a move away from the extended family, which had been symbolised by group and open-couple dances, and a move towards the nuclear family structure, with the (dancing) couple at its centre.

CHAPTER FIVE

Return of the Repressed?
Set Dance, Postmodernity and Community

A flyer advertises a dance holiday in the Spanish island resort of Ibiza, famed for its disco dance clubs. This particular holiday promises 'Sun, Sand, Sea and Sets' and invites the reader to 'join us for the "Craic" in Ibiza'. The set-dance holiday, scheduled to take place in April 2002, was an event in the fifth Fleadh España and provides a good illustration of the popularity of set dance in Ireland at this time.[1] Apart from the holiday abroad, there were many other opportunities for set dancing in cities, towns and villages all over the country. These included classes, set-dance céilís, pub dancing, set-dance weekends, as well as week-long summer schools, most notably the Willie Clancy School in Miltown Malbay, County Clare (see figs 13 and 14). Why did this dance genre, once the most common dance form in rural Ireland, become so popular again fifty years later? And furthermore, was set dance in its more contemporary incarnation 're-invented and re-contextualised in response to social and cultural change' (Snape, 2009, p. 298)?

This chapter contends that the increased popularity of set dance between the 1970s and the mid-1990s reflected significant changes in Irish society, changes that were to affect people's sense of embodied identity, as well as the nature and quality of their relationship to others. The discussion revolves around a consideration of the social and cultural climate of the revival era as well as conversations with dancers about their enjoyment of set dancing. The main argument put forward in this chapter is that set dancing provided participants with a particular sense of community. I use the term 'community' to refer to the informal relationships that dancers build up through set-dance practice, which generates 'a special sense of

communion or commonality that is derived from their shared interests' (Tovey and Share, 2000, p. 336). I suggest that this dance
form, historically associated with the geographical communities of
rural Ireland, was a manifestation of 'cultural stability and continuity' (Buckland, 2001, p. 1) and for some a nostalgic search for the
idealised values of these disappearing places. Equally importantly, it
is claimed, the community generated through set dancing was a new
kind of community and expressed a desire for some of the freedoms
of urban living as well as a resistance to its constraints.

Changing Society, Changing Communities

Set dancing, which had been the most common form of social dancing
for almost two centuries, had suffered a general decline in the 1930s,
though the tradition was kept alive in a few places, most notably West
Cork, Kerry and Clare. According to Tubridy (1994) the causes of the
decline were multiple and included rural migration, clerical hostility,
the creation of, and an increasing popularity of, an alternative
'authentic' canon of Irish dance both before and after national independence in 1922, the suppression of house dancing following the
enforcement of the Public Dance Halls Act in 1935 and, finally,
increased prosperity leading to changing patterns of consumption.
However, the early 1970s saw the 'return of the repressed' in the form
of a revival that gained momentum over the next two decades and was
flourishing at the time of my own research in the mid-1990s.

The set-dance revival coincided with an era of rapid social change
in Ireland. Both the 1960s and 1970s saw a number of major
national developments that were to open Ireland up to outside economic, political and cultural influences. At a cultural level, the
renewed interest in Irish music and dance can be understood as part
of the general folk revival in the 1960s as well as the establishment of
a national television station, Teilifís Éireann, in 1961. At an economic and political level the Lemass–Whitaker policies exposed
Ireland to outside economic influences, including joining the
European Economic Community in 1971. The awareness that
Ireland was now becoming part of a larger world led to a renewed
interest in Irish traditional culture and the values and ways of life
associated with it. For some this interest was motivated by a fear that
Ireland's national culture might be swamped in a larger union of

European states, and for others it was seen as an opportunity to bring a unique national cultural contribution to the enlarged multinational unit. There was also a widely held view that as a nation we were becoming too dependent on British and American popular culture, exemplified for instance in the substantial amount of importation of television programmes from Britain and the USA.

By the mid-1990s these social and cultural changes had intensified. National policy issues, particularly in relation to agriculture and tourism, were affecting rural Ireland profoundly. The weakening of traditional rural communities, the rationalisation of agriculture and the demise of small farms as well as the associated *meitheal oibre* (mutual aid) were all part of this process. The social interconnections of people living within a particular local boundary were in decline, widespread car ownership led to people shopping in towns rather than local villages, many sub-post offices and Garda stations were closed and the introduction of drink-driving laws lessened the frequency with which people visited local pubs. The processes of urbanisation and suburbanisation were also intensifying. In the urban environment too the structures and institutions that had historically underpinned a sense of commonality such as trade unions had weakened (but see Corcoran et al. (2010) for a counter-argument on the isolation of suburban life).

Many of the social and cultural changes taking place from the 1970s to the 1990s were not unique to Ireland but were rather embedded in ongoing global processes. One of the key concerns of writers on the fate of local communities in an increasingly globalised world is isolation and individualisation and a consequent decline in community. A case in point is Putnam's (2000) well-known 'bowling alone' thesis, addressing the relative breakdown of community values in the USA. In addition, developments in communication technologies led to an increase in online/virtual communication and social networking with a corollary decline in the frequency with which people communicated face to face. Another major change in social life was the demise of the 'grand narratives' of the Enlightenment and with it the overturning of fundamental certainties such as religious beliefs. The majority of people were now living in a society where there was no one truth and no fixed or immutable identity. These changes were seen to usher in a new kind of society qualitatively different from the previous one and commonly referred to as 'postmodern' (see Harvey, 1989, and Tovey and Share, 2000, p. 425, in an Irish context). Though the term itself is highly contested, it is useful in the current discussion for helping to understand identity formation in contemporary life. Bauman's (1996) distinction between modern and postmodern identities is helpful. Modern identity, according to Bauman, is characterised by the idea of one's life as a journey that progressively moves towards the goals of selfhood. Postmodern identity, in contrast, describes a situation which is reflexive and in which multiple fragments of identity are constantly and opportunistically in play. These are not mutually exclusive categories but are rather tendencies and I suggest below that set dancers operate with both an essential (modern) and a more reflexive (postmodern) approach to identity. Giddens' (1991, p. 18) concept of 'disembeddedness' is also relevant to the discussion. The era of late modernity (he does not use the prefix 'post') is characterised, according to Giddens, by 'the lifting out of social relations from local contexts and their re-articulation across indefinite tracts of timespace'. Set dancing was partially a reaction to the disembedding process and a desire to bring social relations back into a local context or, in other words, a re-embedding process.

The fact that cultural identities in postmodern societies are no longer based on local geographic communities of the street or the parish can also be seen as positive. Identities are multiple and in forming them people seek out new communities of interest that they are free to leave at any time. People remain members in part because of the emotional satisfaction they derive from common goals or experiences. These new communities provide safe social spaces for identity testing, for empowerment and for learning new skills. They provide opportunities for communication and creativity and 'the realisation of physical, sensuous and intellectual capacities' as well as 'the creation of non-commodity use-values' (Gorz, quoted in Urry, 1995, p. 221). Hast's (1993, p. 21) depiction of the contra dance community in New England is a good example of this new kind of leisure community, based as she affirms on 'interest, "affinity" and experience rather than on more traditional notions of the bounded community characterised by neighbourhood, family relationships, ethnicity, and/or religious affiliation'. Set dance, it is suggested, provides another example of such a community.

Folk Dance and Community

The sets were the most 'authentic' folk dance in Ireland because they were the most commonly danced by ordinary people in rural areas for at least two hundred years (see Brennan, 1999, p. 30). Folk dance itself, because of its 'embodied and collective' style (Norris, 2001, p. 304), is regarded by dance scholars (e.g. Buckland, 2001; Norris, 2001; Cresswell, 2006; Snape, 2009) as generating a sense of belonging to a community which was historically a rural community. It came to be associated with a sense of the collective/communal as opposed to the individual, and of the traditional as opposed to the modern when the term itself was coined in the nineteenth century to differentiate it from other dances forms (see Francmanis, 2002). Cecil Sharp, the figure most associated with the revival of English folk or country dance in the early twentieth century, contrasted it with the ornamented, ostentatious and individualistic style of the formal dances of polite society. Country dance was to embody the unsophisticated style of the 'unlettered' classes amongst whom the dances were thought to have originated (Sharp, quoted in Snape, 2009, pp. 300–1). As characterised by Sharp it was 'a unique instrument for the expression of those ideas that are held and felt collectively, but peculiarly unfitted for the exploitation of personal idiosyncrasies'. As a country dance it was seen as an embodiment of English pastoral values of simplicity, naturalness and collectivity, in that the dancers should do no more than follow the steps exactly as instructed and avoid all expression of individuality. Through its style the dance became an embodied representation of a simple communal form of dance in which the dancer 'should fulfil this purpose effectively and in the simplest and most direct way . . . its style was argued to embody moral virtues . . . and to be alien to those whose experience was limited to contemporary urban and non-traditional popular dances'.

Set Dance and Community

Though far removed in time and place from English country dance as described by Sharp, conversations with set dancers revealed that they too sought and experienced a sense of community 'of simplicity, naturalness and collectivity'. This experience of community was created through both the social context and the kinaesthetics of dance performance. The following discussion is based on conversations with set dancers in the mid-1990s as well as my own experience and observations of set dance around this time. There were four main set-dance venues during the research period, including weekly classes, set-dance céilís, weekend workshops held in various locations outside Dublin, and regular weekly set-dance sessions in a number of city pubs. The dance events consisted of a core group of participants, including musicians, callers and dancers, the latter including a core group of regular dancers, occasional dancers and perhaps a small number of once-off visitors/tourists. The dancers to whom I spoke attended at least one of these dance events regularly at this time and frequently more than one.[2] They were for the most part professional middle-class women and men in the 30–50 age group who lived in Dublin city.[3]

Performance Context and Community

'The performance context itself is a crucial component in creating the collective, providing a purpose for the functioning of the group, and helping to define individual identity' (Hast, 1993, p. 23). Hast's observations on contra dancing were echoed in conversations with set dancers. Of particular importance to set dancers was the welcoming and friendly demeanour of the participants in the dance events. Asked about what attracted her to set dance Mary replied:

> I think the music and the dancing. That's one thing but I don't think that's the prime reason . . . the primary motive is just 'the craic' that goes on . . . but I think there has to be more than that . . . I think it's just the whole scene around you and they are all people that are similar really to your own.

Mary's primary motive for doing set dancing, 'the craic', implies convivial social interaction and a sense of exuberance and spontaneity usually associated with music, lively conversation and banter. In contrasting the set-dance ambience favourably with that of disco, Kate reported that:

> [I] . . . hated going to a disco, low lights, loud music, darkness or almost darkness, you couldn't see people, you couldn't have a decent conversation with them and I never really enjoyed that. I preferred set dancing . . . it's much more sociable in that you can talk to somebody and you're not blasted out by the live music . . . it's usually a nice, bright airy and roomy atmosphere.

Some dancers expressed a belief that set dancing was a great leveller. For instance Margaret thought that social class/status differences are abolished:

> Meeting people from various backgrounds . . . people in set dancing . . . it's totally irrelevant what somebody's economic or social background is . . . you're in there together . . . very rarely do people actually end up discussing issues or debating things, your mind is not important, it's very much yourself and you're taken as a person rather than as a just kind of what your cv says, you could be mixing with brain surgeons or you could be mixing with absolutely anybody, from any kind of a background, and you'll never know and it's not important, and people can form friendships and relationships based on their enjoyment of the music and dance which I think is fantastic . . . it's a classless sort of activity really.

Margaret's belief in the levelling effect of the dance activity is well captured in Turner's (1974, p. 238) concept of 'communitas', which refers to 'rituals in which egalitarian and co-operative behaviour is characteristic, and in which secular distinctions of rank, office, and status are temporarily in abeyance or regarded as irrelevant'. The quote also conveys a sense that interaction confers anonymity.[4]

Helen also speaks of the friendliness, the opportunity for talking and the ease of communication with other dancers. She, too, contrasts the atmosphere with that of disco:

> it doesn't matter who you are, everybody talks to each other, you know people by name, you don't have to know what they do, they're just nice to one another . . . if you go to a disco, for a start, you can't talk to anyone at a disco.

Emma was also attracted by the friendliness and the variety of people:

> They're very friendly, old and young . . . and there is a mix, there's a good mix and everyone is so friendly . . . might know their first name but I wouldn't know their second name, what their surname are . . . or where they're from or anything else, but everyone seems to get on well.

Some dancers moved beyond the desire to remain anonymous to become involved in wider networks of interaction outside the dance event:

1. Postcard 'the Ould Irish Jig' (*Laurence Publisher, Dublin, 1904*; Copyright © Mary Evans Picture Library).

THE OULD IRISH JIG.

"Then a fig for the new fashioned waltzes
Imported from Spain and from France,
And a fig for the thing called the polka,
Our own Irish jig we will dance."

2. Cover of programme for Feis na Mumhan, 1910 (Courtesy of *Irish Traditional Music Archive*).

3. Colleens Dancing, Ballymaclinton, Franco–British Exhibition, London, 1908 (Courtesy of the *Belfast Telegraph*).

4. Cover image, 'A Handbook of Irish Dances' (Courtesy of *Irish Traditional Music Archive*).

5. Newspaper headline (Courtesy of *Irish Newspaper Archives*).

6. Rainbow 'Ballroom of Romance', Glenfarne, Co. Leitrim, 2008 (Copyright © Kenneth Allen, http//:creativecommons.org).

7. Granada Dance Hall, Granard, Co. Longford (Copyright © Richard Webb, http//:creativecommons.org).

CARRICK - ON - SHANNON
ROWING CLUB.

GRAND CARNIVAL DANCE
Will be held in
GAIETY,
CARRICK - ON - SHANNON
(UNDER ABOVE AUSPICES)
—On—
Friday Night, 9th November, 1934
Dancing at 10.30 sharp.

CARNIVAL NOVELTIES.
VALUABLE SPOT DANCE PRIZES

Music by Bert Flynn and His Six-Piece
No. 1 Band.

TICKETS ... ... 5/- EACH
(including tax).
Supper Extra; catering under Gaiety
Management.

Specially prepared and sprung floor;
modern and up-to-date accommodation
and lighting; and central heating.

8. Newspaper advertisement for dance, 1934 (Courtesy of *Irish Newspaper Archives*).

A GRAND CONCERT and
Dramatic Entertainment
Will be held in
Mooney's Hall, Drumshanbo,
—On—
SUNDAY, 11th NOVEMBER
" The Lad from Largymore "
Will be staged by the
DRUMSHANBO DRAMATIC TROOP

LEO ROWSOME
Will be in attendance to give selections
on the Uilleann Pipes both at concert
and ceilidh.

Songs, Step-Dancing and Recitations
will also be a feature of the night.

Proceeds in aid of the Corderay Football
Field.

ADMISSION ... ... 2/- and 1/-

A CEILIDH WILL FOLLOW
Admission, 6d.

9. Newspaper advertisement for Concert and Ceilidh, 1934 (Courtesy of *Irish Newspaper Archives*).

10. Dancing in the Crystal Ballroom, Dublin, 1954 (Courtesy of *Fáilte Ireland*).

11. Roadside Dancing, Kilcoran, Cahir, Co. Tipperary, 1958 (Courtesy of the *Irish Photo Archive/Lensmen Photographic Archive*, www.irishphotoarchive.ie).

12. Roscommon Men's Association Dinner Dance, Gresham Hotel, Dublin, 1958 (Courtesy of the *Irish Photo Archive/Lensmen Photographic Archive*, www.irishphotoarchive.ie)

13. Set dancing, Miltown Malbay, Co. Clare, 2002
(Copyright © 2013 Bill Lynch, *Set Dancing News*).

14. Set dancing, Curracloe, Co. Wexford, 2003
(Copyright © Bill Lynch, *Set Dancing News*).

15. Irish Cailíní, image from Francis O'Neill's *Irish Minstrels and Musicians*
(Courtesy of the *Irish Traditional Music Archive*).

16. Competitors, Australian Irish Dancing Championships, 2012
(Copyright © *Milton Baar, Media Images*).

17. Watching the Australian Irish Dancing Championships, 2012 (Copyright Milton Baar, Media Images).

18. Newspaper advertisement for dance in New York City (Courtesy of the *Joe Burke Archive, National University of Ireland, Galway*).

19. *Riverdance* (Photo: Jack Hartin Copyright © Abhann Productions, 2007).

A scene from Riverdance. Composed by Bill Whelan, Produced by Moya Doherty, Directed by John McColgan
© Abhann Productions Photographer Clark James Mishler

20. *Riverdance* (Photo: James Mishler Copyright © Abhann Productions).

21. Front cover of brochure for music and dance show (Courtesy of *The Merry Ploughboy Irish Music Pub Dublin*, www.mpbpub.com).

it's the part about the engagement with other people around a common activity that you all love . . . I would say that it goes beyond the class in the sense that we do other things together but they're all around set dancing . . . like we all go to the pub afterwards. (Brian)

This supports Hast's (p. 23) findings on contra dance that 'participants are drawn into wider networks of communication, activity, and association that often grow and develop outside and beyond the dance'.

Intergenerational communication and continuity were seen to be promoted through set dancing because of its age inclusiveness.[5] In Paul's words, 'It's such a terrific community thing and it brings in all ages.' Seamus thought that the age mix contributed complementary styles and energies to the dance event:

set dancing can be quite wild or it can be extremely tame and I'd say regimented, if you watch older people dancing, people who have been life-long set dancers, they can get through any number of sets with seemingly effortless grace, some of them, and don't seem to expend an awful lot of energy . . . it's because they are very practised dancers whereas maybe younger dancers, myself included, throw an awful lot of energy around.

Brian was attracted to the idea of the continuity of connection with this community into his older age:

It is a way for me over time particularly as I get older to continue to be active and to be connected to people . . . and for me the notion that there is a community of people there that share something real engaging physical, mental, social, spiritual, if you will, guys from down the country dancing . . . and they are respected . . . older versions of me or something so that's nice, you're part of something that remains.

While many of the pleasures of set dancing were equally shared by men and women, some appeared to be gender specific. Women, for instance, reported a feeling of security that they would not have experienced in other dance situations and which afforded them, in turn, a sense of personal freedom and control. Mary, for example, spoke of the freedom to be flirtatious in a safe environment:

Half the fun in a set is the winking and the nodding and the messin' that goes on which is total flirtation – that's half the fun of it – but it's all very safe, you know that there is not going to be someone at the door waiting for you, it's very false in a way but it's very safe and it's fun . . . I think the fact that you can walk away easily, the time limit is almost defined for every interaction . . . and everybody knows the rules.

Margaret, too, contrasts the formal conventions surrounding set dancing with the less rule-bound and, hence, more risky behaviour at a disco:

And another nice thing is that in a set dance it's organised in a sense that you know when you can leave the person . . . if you are dancing with somebody that you don't like, officially at the end of four figures or whatever, that's it, you can go and say 'thank you very much' . . . whereas in a disco situation if you're dancing with someone you don't want to be with, it can go on forever . . . you're not sure when the point will come when you can leave him.

Both Mary and Margaret express the sense of relative freedom they felt in their freedom to flirt and their ability to escape from an undesirable dance partner if they so wished. These comments can be understood in the context of the legacy of the greater control over public dance spaces by men historically and which they perceived as ongoing in other dance situations such as disco.

Women also spoke favourably of set dancing with regard to the 'presentation of self' (Goffman, 1959), particularly in relation to image and dress:

They [people at the disco] were also very conscious of how they look and their image . . . set dancing you just don't have time and at the end of an afternoon or an evening set dancing most people look horrendous anyway [laughs] and it's a great leveller, people sort of laugh at themselves and at other people – 'look at the state of me here!' – so it's a great way of – how would I describe it? – it tears away the superficiality of most dancing . . . when you stink to high heaven, well, there's no problem there . . . you're accepted completely. (Margaret)

Margaret's contrasting of the 'presentation of self' in disco and set dance takes on board the importance of image in certain dance contexts. She sees set dance as debunking image consciousness and as offering a more natural, unaffected and authentic 'presentation of self'. Her comments illustrate the ideology of 'naturalness' associated with folk dance and echo Sharp's (quoted in Snape, p. 301) belief that folk dancing is 'not the place for the display of those self-conscious airs and graces, fanciful posings and so forth'.

Dancers' comments clearly indicated that the social context of set dancing was regarded as sociable and inclusive, and created an ambience in which dancers could feel at ease, accepted and safe.[6] It created a sense of community, with its emphasis on the collective, the simple, the natural, and on continuity. To some degree too it was a new community for women, enabling them to exercise a degree of control over the nature and extent of social interaction within the community.

Group Dancing and Connectivity

Dance scholars and anthropologists alike attest to the fact that group dancing generates and maintains community solidarity at both a symbolic and kinaesthetic level (see, for example, Radcliffe-Brown, 1964; Rust, 1969; Boas, 1972; Lange, 1975; Douglas, 1976; Cowan, 1990; Bottomley, 1992; Tabar, 2005). The dancers to whom I spoke confirmed the distinctive and multi-dimensional appeal of dancing in a full set of eight people. They reported feeling a strong sense of the collective created through a range of performance elements including communication, physical contact, sharing embodied knowledge, cooperative effort, correct movement, and visual metaphor – elements that are in practice, and in conversation with dancers, interlinked, but separately enumerated here for the sake of clarity.

Dancers' comments support Cowan's (1990, p. 20) observation that:

> To be a participant in the dance is to be in (and with) the group ... The dance, graphically suggesting a collectivity bound by shared knowledge, skill and physical connection, is considered an apt metaphor for the community itself.

COMMUNICATION

Dancers noted the opportunities for communication, verbal and non-verbal, that present themselves:

> You *are* communicating with people that you are dancing with, so, as I say, it may not be verbal all the time because it's not easy, but it might be a nod or a wink ... there are some dances where that particular movement is part of the figure ... for example in

the Corofin Plain Set . . . you nod to the person opposite you, so there is that kind of communication there. (Kate)

Brian comments on the sense of awareness of, and engagement with, dance partners:

> [there is] something real important about rotating partners, because when you do that you are engaging with people *all* the time . . . and everybody does it and you have to be aware of other people, [in rock and roll] there's no interdependence, [in set dance] you'll get carried and you'll help someone else, so I think that's what it is, and then you see people a month later and you talk about some incident that happened . . . that you all know about, that's all shared . . . it's in everybody's experience.

Here we see how the sharing of the performance generates shared memories that create a sense of the collective.

Communication through physical contact was also a major source of enjoyment. For Cormac:

> set dancing was doing something very physical at the same time . . . there is the rhythm aspect of it which I really enjoy as well and there's also the physical contact aspect of it which I think is important.

In contrast to set dance, he goes on to reflect on the physical (and psychological) barriers imposed in disco:

> There, a lot of barriers between people are actually built up in these situations because when you dance with somebody, it's on this basis, 'I will dance with her or I won't dance with her' depending on whether I really like them or not . . . not on the basis of whether you actually want to *dance* with them . . . I can often see a high level of frustration in the end . . . if absolutely no contact is made, so instead of breaking down physical barriers between people I think it can actually really build them up and exacerbate any kind of tensions or frustrations that people have going into a place where they are already quite nervous.

Margaret notes that:

> You have the physical contact of being with somebody, holding another person . . . a lot of people who don't have physical contact . . . it's the only time that they get a chance to 'get a hoult' of somebody [laughs] . . . it's a kind of safe way of still

having some physical intimacy without the kind of, you know, attachment or whatever.

Margaret's observation seems to display a tension between intimacy and detachment. On the one hand her references to physical contact might be seen as an example of the communicative body which adopts a 'dyadic relationship with others who join in the dance' and 'implies an associatedness which goes beyond one's own body and extends to the body of the other(s)' (Frank, 1991, p. 80). Alternatively, it could be seen as a case of 'intimate anonymity' (Abbott, 1987, pp. 164–5) providing an opportunity for physical closeness during the performance but without further commitment outside and beyond the dance (see Hast, 1993, p. 26).

ACCOMPLISHMENT IN CO-OPERATIVE EFFORT

Dancers talked about their enjoyment of collaborating with other dancers in the set. Eileen referred to the sense of achievement she felt in this kind of co-operative effort:

> I actually like the feeling of achievement that you get . . . from being with somebody who can dance . . . it's like an achievement, you've done something well – there has been a contact with somebody, you've done it as a unit – it's not just yourself and not even in a couple. There is also a solidarity in the set . . . that you'll . . . help each other out, a feeling of accomplishment.

Seamus too commented that 'It was a very, very sociable thing, it was kind of like co-operative learning' and spoke of the 'tremendous sensation' of the set moving as a unitary body:

> a tremendous level of satisfaction if you're in a set that's dancing very well, that's really in time with the music and I suppose nearly moving as one, that's a tremendous sensation.

Seamus's enjoyment was also based on a contagion effect that made the learning appear effortless. Ethnomusicologist John Blacking (1977, p. 4) explains that these techniques of the body 'are not entirely learnt *from* others so much as discovered through others'. He uses the term 'proto-ritual' for this process, which he sees as 'a shared somatic state of the social body that generates special kinds of feelings and apparently spontaneous movement and interaction between bodies in space and time' (p. 14). Helen speaks of the pleasure she got from familiarity with her partners' dancing style, the group element and equal levels of dancing skill:

> You might get into a set where you know everybody – you know the way they dance, you know the way they move – and you get such a buzz . . . eight people in the set at the same level . . . to me it's fantastic!

Brian also speaks of the dual process of communicating and learning how to complement his partner's moves:

> the other dancing doesn't have any of that so you have no aware-ness of other people in the real sense . . . with this [set dance] you do and everybody is so individual . . . there is a woman who is a good friend of ours . . . we just do [The Lancers] perfectly together . . . she moves her feet differently from than I do . . . and that's true of everybody, the way the body moves in relation to you and how you fit together. And particularly swinging . . . there's something just wonderful about that, where you get the timing right and you start going faster and faster. There's a feeling of closeness . . . it's like you're taking off.

The dancers' comments are testimony to an embodied knowledge of dancing partners, confirming Norris's (2001, p. 11) claim that:

> Specific knowledge and qualities are exchanged through bodily participation in folk dance events, coming from the music, the postures, physical contact, and social context . . . The body . . . recognises and receives communication directly from other bodies, allowing posture, gesture, and imagery to develop as alter-native means of transmitting knowledge and feeling of various states of being . . . In folk dance it can be seen in the subtle move-ment of a shoulder to correct another's dance step, a glance that communicates more than idle flirtation, or an embellishment that expresses clearly a state of freedom of the body in sure knowledge of the dance.

FLOW

Many of the quotes about dancing with a partner or partners convey the sense of being grounded and physically connected to partners but at the same time of being elevated and elated. Brian talks of a feeling of elation and connectedness in a set:

> I have a real feel of elation, particularly when you've finished a figure at high speed and come to a stop . . . I don't know how to

describe it . . . the only thing I can think of that is parallel to it is the feelings that I would have in playing sports in a team but that's not quite the same thing . . . in sport you are always competing . . . but here nobody loses so . . . when it's right, [you are] connected to everybody.

Others too express feelings of exhilaration and lightness:

Exhilaration, I suppose, isn't it? . . . of enjoyment . . . you know when you meet a really good dancer you just actually, you feel on air, don't you? A lovely feeling of lightness . . . I love it. (Angela)

When you are dancing with someone there are certain kinds of energy fields or electrical fields, that come from how the person is, it's almost like an aura. (Peter)

The terms 'lightness,' 'exhilaration', 'taking off' and 'aura' used in the extracts above point to the peak pleasures of group dancing and have been variously described in the literature as 'flow', as 'being danced' and as transcendence. Many dance scholars have drawn attention to this feeling. Norris (2001, p. 117), for example, explains the feeling of 'being danced' in the following way:

The repetition of figures in dance reinforces the association between feeling and movement, causing the experience of dance to live more strongly in the body itself . . . At the other end [of the spectrum] is 'mindfulness', or 'presence', which is mindfulness or presence in the body. In dance, one of the most mindful experiences is the rare peak experience of 'being danced', where knowledge and agency are experienced as coming from outside the self.

Both Csikszentmihalyi (1991) and Connerton (1989) use the term 'flow' to describe these feelings of pleasure. Csikszentmihalyi sees it as having a mental source, while Connerton (p. 94) sees it as emanating from 'habit memory':

By exercise the body comes to coordinate an increasing range of muscular activities in an increasingly automatic way, until awareness retreats, the movement flows 'involuntarily', and there occurs a firm and practiced sequence of acts which take their fluent course.

Whether the source is bodily habit, as claimed by Connerton, or a mental capacity, as claimed by Csikzentmihalyi, the effect is the same: a sense of being both grounded and elevated and of being within and outside the body simultaneously. This sensory experience generates both a heightened sense of the individual self and of collectivity and corresponds to the feelings accompanying religious ritual as outlined by Émile Durkheim (1915). Drawing on Durkheim's insights on the link between religious practice and social solidarity, Norris (2001, p. 117) draws parallels between dancing and religious ritual in creating community:

> the correspondence between the posture and the inner state is learned, and inevitably learned not in isolation, but within a community of dancers. Part of the intent of ritual performance is to establish a common practice. Religious leaders have known for millennia that when people undergo a discipline together or harmonise their actions, they will feel themselves to be part of something larger.

The findings here in relation to set dance confirm Hast's (1993, p. 26) observations that these experiences of 'high' points and transcendence in contra dance can lead to a sense of loyalty that in turn leads to a sense of community.

CORRECT MOVEMENT

A number of dancers made reference to correct movement, as in comments such as 'getting it right', 'being with somebody who can dance', or 'if you're in a set that's dancing very well . . . that's really in time with the music' and so on. The emphasis on keeping in time and getting it right is a feature of folk dance performance in general, as explained by Norris (2001, p. 118):

> Unlike modern performative dance, which is idiosyncratic and 'self'-centered, certain types of folk dance require that one insert oneself as little as possible, conforming instead to a pattern that the other dancers are also attempting to embody. Participation in the dance event calls for adherence to forms not of one's own choosing: the music demands that figures be executed in a specific time frame, and the figures of a particular dance are set combinations.

Angela remarks on the 'lovely feeling' from adhering to the dance pattern and time-frame:

> There's a lovely feeling too to getting it right, isn't there? And getting the dance done as it ought to be danced and getting it kind of . . . getting round it in time.

A related element in the dancers' enjoyment was the structure of the dance itself. At times this was inferred but Cormac made explicit reference to the dance form itself as a major source of enjoyment:

> the form is what people really enjoy and I think it does come back to the idea of form in lots of things – people need form and through form people develop ... I think there is so much ... postmodern [inaudible] breaking up form, but almost these people swimming with nothing to hang on to at all, more than anything I think it can be very disorientating.

He goes on to elaborate by contrasting set dancing to disco:

> I think that set dancing and disco dancing are almost completely opposed to each other in terms of style and form and content. I think that a disco atmosphere creates all sorts of boundaries ... the type of dancing where one can never be good at it ... so it's not really a question of being good or bad but deciding what way *you* want to dance because there is no actual form.

Timmy also thought that it was more fun to do set dance because of the rules:

> I'd much rather the set dancing by far because unless you're a really natural dancer ... dancing is hard ... there are no rules, you just have to sort of follow your own ... so I always think [set dancing] more fun than a night club.

For Cormac and Timmy the attraction of rules/form in set dance can be seen as creating a sense of the collective for dancers. However, the remarks appear to be nuanced differently. Angela seems to want to 'get it right' so as to coordinate with other members of the set, whereas for Cormac and Timmy the rules act as a frame for their dancing, thereby enabling them to avoid the potential awkwardness, self-consciousness or embarrassment of dancing free form.[7] Whatever the motivation for adherence to the rules, it is clear that set dancers need to conform to a predetermined pattern in the correct tempo to be able to perform the dance well. In so doing they privilege the collective over the individual. However, the set-dance form, combining as it does group, couple and some individual sequences, allows for the symbolic expression of both individuality and community. Community, I propose, is represented through the group elements, the nuclear family through the paired elements, and the individual through the solo sequences. Since the latter are minimal, it is the group elements that remain predominant in the overall performance.

VISUAL METAPHOR

Dance as metaphor for community was clearly articulated when dancers talked about their favourite dances. The fifth figure of the Clare Lancers was frequently mentioned in this regard. In this particular figure the line-up, side step, and advance retire movements are transformed by joining hands with members of the adjoining set to form several continuous lines of dancers so that each individual set becomes part of one large set, uniting the whole hall of dancers. Dancers talked about the way in which the visual and the kinaesthetic merge to produce this sense of the collective:

> to look at it [Clare Lancers] from a balcony, for example in Seapoint in Salthill, the international weekend, it's just amazing, you just see a sea of people and they are moving together . . . it's just unreal and it's very nice. (Kate)

Nuala also spoke of its attraction:

> I love the line-up, the military line-up and I love that . . . it's just so neat and it looks lovely . . . opportunity to look at it from a balcony . . . it looks lovely . . . it's so uniform.

Though the appeal is here based on a sense of order, the reference to military uniformity again conveys a sense of collective movement (see McNeill, 1997). Margaret explicitly associates the figure with a sense of community:

> I love the Clare Lancers because . . . at the end when people hold hands together the whole hall can hold hands at the same time . . . so you get a great feeling of community from that one.

Dancers' comments resonate with Cowan's (1990, p. 226) interpretation of the dancing line in Northern Greece as 'a utopian image of the collective at its most joyous, sensuous and orderly best'.

The pleasures of set dancing were multiple, as indicated in the dancers' comments above. They spoke of the sense of achievement in collaborating as a group, of getting to know people through the physicality and proximity of dancing, the ease of communicating with partners verbally and non-verbally, learning through sharing the dance, of the experience of 'flow', elation and transcendence, and of the visual metaphors of community that they enjoy. All of these pleasures generated a sense of embodied community. This community fits the model of the new community of interests outlined earlier, facilitating as it did communication, physical and sensuous enjoyment, and the creation of non-commodity use values.

Rural Romanticism and its Contradictions

In addition to creating a community of interests, set dancing was also associated with the more local and traditional geographic community. A number of the women dancers[8] to whom I spoke saw rural Ireland as a repository of an authentic set-dance tradition and expressed a desire to be part of it. Places singled out for mention in idealised terms were those where set dancing had survived and continued to be part of local culture, such as Clare, Kerry and West Cork. Margaret talked about her initial introduction to, and motivation for, taking up set dancing in the following anecdote:

> My first experience of set dancing was in Milltown Malbay years ago in 1983 . . . I didn't know what set dancing was at the time, I'd never heard of it, seen it or anything . . . I saw this vision in the street of eight people of various ages . . . and what struck me was there was an old man, I don't know what age he was, late sixties maybe, or early seventies, dancing furiously with a *young* one . . . with a loose flowing skirt and hair . . . a real Irish colleen . . . and the two of them were tearing into this wild furious dance . . . and I just thought: 'God, it's incredible' . . . for me it sort of . . . it was some kind of a symbol of the vitality of the Irish spirit, that's the only way I could describe it . . . the Atlantic Ocean itself is the vitality and the passion of Irish people . . . and that lashing of the waves against the rock is just what I see in set dancing.

A number of romanticised motifs are linked, the wildness of the dance with the wildness of the landscape, to produce a seamless association between the natural, the expressive and the passionate.

Some dancers were connected to rural Ireland through parents or relatives, as Anne remarked when explaining the appeal of polkas:

> I just love polkas . . . I would be drawn to it anyway because I come from West Cork . . . my father does . . . that's how I feel I belong there.

Eileen also spoke of the distinctive set dancing that she had seen down the country:

> I love Kerry you know, anything to do with Kerry, I just love . . . I have this vision . . . I mean the best dancers I have ever seen in my life down in Connell's pub in Knocknagree . . . and that's my image of them doing polkas down there . . . and that's what I want . . . they're not actually dancing on the ground, they're dancing on the air . . . that's where I want to be.

Later in the discussion she speaks of her desire to dance indefinitely:

> I often think it's something I could do for my life . . . the granny when I'm still in my zimmer frame [general laughter] . . . again to go back to that famous night in Knocknagree, in Danny Connell's . . . with these people dancing up in the air . . . ninety-year-olds dancing the same dance . . . they were doing it at a slower pace and everything but I thought that was wonderful.

The attraction of generational continuity mentioned by Eileen was echoed by Orla when speaking about the harmony of dancers who have been long-time partners, a phenomenon which she believes was exclusive to rural Ireland:

> It's lovely to see couples . . . go down the country like you might see a couple . . . they're married or whatever, they've danced together for years and they dance exactly the same . . . couples in their sixties now who've gone out dancing together every Saturday night for the last twenty years . . . I mean you wouldn't have that up in Dublin . . . that is just fantastic to watch.

The dancers' comments above confirm Raymond Williams' (1973) claim that the dominant image of the country is as a repository of organic community and authentic folk culture. It also resonates with Jonathan Culler's (1981) view that one of the charactistics of modernity is the belief that authenticity has been lost and exists only in the past. The rural romanticism is not just related to the landscape and the people but to the activity of set dancing itself. As Snape (2009, p. 297) observes, folk dance may be considered as an embodied performance of a perceived tradition and is representational of values attached to an imagined past. There was also an admiration of those rural communities where the generations can socialise together and where people of all ages are given the opportunity to dance.[9] For some of the women set dancing symbolised an idealised rural community characterised by intergenerational continuity, contact and communication.

Despite the romantic imagery that some women associated with rural set dancing, there appeared to be a disjuncture between their own experience of dancing and representations of set dancing in the country and the city. While they wished to immerse themselves in the traditional community, in some respects they perceived it as belonging to another time and place. This paradox is apparent in responses to a question about their image of the type of people who do set dancing. Here a less flattering representation emerged:

> My first impressions always at any of these workshops is 'Oh, my God, will you look at this lot?!' [laughs] . . . I remember my first workshop in Galway and I looked around the room and there was little old grannies in Aran cardigans . . . and they were all practising the steps and I thought 'This is sad . . . oh, my God!' . . . all the square people of Ireland, you know . . . were kind of gathered together and I just thought 'no, thank you . . . but the minute you get into doing the activity, that changes completely . . . I mean it looks from the outside total boredom . . . but once you get involved in the actual doing of it, you know, it changes. (Margaret)

Here we see the image of the female set dancer transmute from the real Irish colleen to 'little old grannies in Aran cardigans', from a representation which connotes beauty and freedom to one which is linked to being drab and outdated. It is also worth noting the perceived paradox between the image and the experience of the dance: while one might love dancing, one does not wish to be associated with the stereotyped image of it. She continued on in a similar vein to give an even more negative image of the typical set dancer:

> The female national teacher . . . men who may be . . . conservative . . . nowhere else to go . . . didn't make it at the discos [laughs] . . . people who are separated are coming back in to meet people again . . . an air of need or loneliness sometimes.

Margaret's reluctance to be associated with such a conservative and needy group leads to a tension between her own self-image and the one she has of her dance associates:

> I look at my friends and we're doing it but we're really not that type . . . and yet if they are doing it they are becoming set-dancing

types . . . but maybe they feel that they don't want to identify themselves with the old image that set dancing is about . . . sometimes I go to céilís and I'm totally depressed . . . I look at a roomful of post-menopausal women, single women . . . the blouse is buttoned up around their head . . . and the long skirt and the brown tights and I go 'Oh, God, is this going to be me? And I start panicking.

Finally, she reassures herself by acknowledging that a variety of people do set dancing:

And then, on other occasions you go and there's a younger set of people or whatever or younger at heart . . . you don't get that feeling . . . but I suppose there's a mix of people doing set dancing.

Eileen makes a similar observation about the contradictions which she perceives between image and involvement:

The first night I went into the Ierne it caused me all sorts of 'God, I'm not going to the Ierne' [tone of mock incredulity accompanied by general laughter] . . . and even into the Merchant [Dublin pub]. I would never have gone to the Merchant in a fit before last year . . . even the bloody mural on the outside of the Merchant, people with skirts on down to here . . . you look at the mural . . . talk about an ancient stereotype of set dancing . . . women in long skirts down to their toes . . . get inside and it's totally different.

Later in the conversation Eileen recounted that her teenage daughter associated set dancing with the country and regarded it as totally outdated – 'out of the Ark':

Sometimes I'd be tryin' to practise my steps at home on the floor [and her daughter would say] 'Jesus, she's off again' . . . she [daughter] was in Mayo last weekend . . . thinks it's the ends of the earth . . . ten-year-old hairstyles and ten-year-old clothes . . . that's her perception of it, you know . . . that would have been my perception.

Timmy, who is of Irish parentage and spent the first ten years of his life in the USA, cites the old-fashioned image of set dancing as the reason his friends avoid it:

Certainly I'd never be able to get anyone in the pubs to go dancing and probably some see it as old-fashioned too, they would rather be going to a night club than a set dance which is, maybe looks old-fashioned, which is old-fashioned really . . . I mean when we were up in Drumcondra, they had tea, cups of tea, and barmbrack halfway through the dance.

The references to cups of tea and barmbrack, grannies in Aran cardigans, the brown tights, the blouse buttoned up around their heads, the ten-year-old hairstyles and clothes, all these negative and stereotypical images of set dancers as lonely, conservative, outdated, desperate, point to a clash between images of set dance in the country and the city. Here again we witness the tensions between traditional notions of rural communities as the repository of communal values but, when transposed to the city – the locus of the modern and contemporary – as outmoded and undesirable.

Between Old and New Communities

Set dance in the Ireland of the 1990s, I have argued, can be seen as an expression of a longing for community. It flourished in the embryonic years of the Celtic Tiger, an era of rapid social change due to the processes of urbanisation and globalisation and developments in communication technologies (mobile phone, online/digital). The combined effect of these processes was a relative decline in the sense of community, including face-to-face social interaction that in turn affected people's personal identity in terms of their sense of embodiment and relationship to others. Set dancing was a way of offsetting these processes and re-embedding the local by creating a sense of the collective through both the social context of the dance events as well as through the dance performance itself. Dancers' accounts emphasised the pleasures of the collective: face-to-face communication and co-operation, egalitarianism and inclusiveness that were perceived to be germane to the dance. Set dancing, I have argued, was a way of performing resistance to a society in which the values of individualism appeared to be taking precedence over those of community. For some, this community had a mythic quality in that it was a place-based geographic community of a rural Ireland believed to be in decline.

Crucially, though, the type of community sought, which in some ways resembled the traditional rural community, was also very different from it. It was a community in which individual agency and choice were combined with collective demands. It functioned in the same way as Urry's 'community of interests', providing dancers with a space in which they could communicate, learn new skills, experiment with social identity and express themselves in an aesthetically and sensually pleasing way. Set-dance practice, therefore, can be seen to bring into being a combination of older/traditional and newer communities of interest. The community the dancers created provided them with a balance between commonality and individuality, between sociability and anonymity, between structure and agency, and between the country and the city. It is proposed that the continuous negotiation and 'strategic flexibility' (Hall, 1990, p. 226) between these binary forms may be seen as a feature of the postmodern sense of identity.

CHAPTER SIX

Dancing the Diaspora
Ethnicity and Cultural Memory

The emigrant Irish like to dance and to party, or at least so the popular representations would have us believe. Note, for example, the scene in the Hollywood film *Titanic* in which Leonardo diCaprio, playing a poor Irish emigrant, escorts the rich upper-class girl below deck where the steerage passengers, also Irish, are having a party. Nuala O'Connor in her book *Bringing It All Back Home* (1991) points to the wild abandon and joyful exuberance of their dancing in stark contrast with the stiffly formal manner of the occupants of the ship's upper deck. While we may be sceptical about the authenticity of Hollywood representations, the extract from the diary of emigrant John J. McClancy, written on his voyage from Queenstown to New York in 1881, confirms the portrayal of the emigrant Irish as lovers of dance. Dancing, he wrote, was the favoured way of passing time on-board ship: 'About eve . . . we had music and dance of all kinds we had great fun in the Germans the way they dance is wheeling around always like we would dance a polka.' And 'When we come up in the morning we don't go down until night the boys and girls are to and fro over the deck we have great games dancing and singing' (quoted in O'Connor, 1991, p. 65). Fintan O'Toole (1997, p. 144) also attests to the popularity of dance before embarkation from Cobh, the port from which Irish emigrants set out on their journey to the New World:

> the cheap boarding houses where the steerage class passengers waited for their passage, became notoriously overcrowded. For those left without a bed, there was, however, a well-known device for getting one. For a few pence, you could get a musician to come in off the street, and strike up a lively tune. Some of those in bed would be unable to resist the urge to get up and dance. And

while they reeled around the floor, you could make a dash for the
bed. At worst, you could lie down for as long as the dancing
continued. At best, if you were strong enough, possession was
nine points of the law.

Whether during the journey to a new land or in the land of
settlement itself, historical accounts attest to the importance of dance
as a means of expression for the Irish diaspora. Its practice became a
distinctive marker of Irish ethnic identity, especially in those
countries to which substantial numbers of Irish migrated, such as
Britain, North America, Australia and New Zealand (see Cullinane,
1997) (see fig. 15). Its current vibrancy is testament to its enduring
role in maintaining this sense of ethnic identity into the twenty-first
century (see figs 16 and 17). Indeed Yu-Chen Lin (2010) claims that
it was the dancers of the diaspora who preserved Irish dance better
than the nation-state itself.

The role of dance in shaping ethnic identities amongst the Irish
diaspora is the subject of this chapter. Ethnic identity is generally
associated with a sense of belonging to a particular place of origin
regarded as home, and the symbolic, if not physical, return to that
homeland. It is in Brah's (1996, p. 192) words 'a mythic place of
desire . . . a place of no return even if it is possible to visit . . . the
place of "origin"'. Both identity and the idea of home are generated
through mobility and movement. This is doubly so for a diaspora, as
they are involved in two kinds of mobility, the migration process
itself and movement through dance. According to Rapport and
Dawson (1998, p. 27) there is currently 'a recognition that not only
can one be at home in movement, but that movement can be one's
very home'. They draw on John Berger's description of the world of
travellers, of labour migrants, exiles and commuters, and of how, for
them, home comes to be found 'in a routine set of practices, a
repetition of habitual interactions, in styles of dress and address, in
memories and myths, in stories carried around in one's head'. Dance
involves all of these elements.

The ritual performance of dance engages with collective memory,
which plays a crucial role in creating and sustaining an 'imagined
homeland' for the diaspora. Drawing again on Connerton's (1989, p.
72) concept of 'habit memory', dance can be seen as having an
embodied mnemonic effect. Our bodies, according to Connerton,
'keep the past . . . in an entirely effective form in their continuing

ability to perform certain skilled actions . . . In habitual memory the past is, as it were, sedimented in the body.' In outlining how memory is sedimented, he distinguishes between two sets of practices, one of which is an incorporating practice such as dance, which involves 'messages that a sender or senders impart by means of their own current bodily activity, the transmission occurring only during the time that their bodies are present to sustain that particular activity'. The other practice he refers to (p. 73) as an inscribing practice which consists of the storing and retrieving of information 'long after the human organism has stopped informing'. Dance memory operates in both forms.

This chapter addresses two main identity functions of dance in the diasporic context. One is a sense of ethnic identity based on the positionality of the Irish amongst other ethnic groups and on the meanings of 'Irishness' in circulation in these multi-ethnic communities. In other words, it refers to the meanings of 'Irishness' ascribed by other individuals and groups. The other is a sense of identification with Irishness by the dancers themselves. The latter is based on the building of ethnic communities through dance in their host country as well as an emotional sense of connection with home/land through the operation of cultural memory.

Constructing Ethnicity: Irish Dance in North America

Dance was performed by the Irish in the USA in at least three distinctive public domains: on the American stage, in dancing schools and competitions, and in the Irish dancehall scene, and I draw on evidence from each of these areas to explore how dancing performed ethnicity. It is likely that Irish dance was introduced to America by pre-Famine migrants as early as the late eighteenth century. We know that Irish dancemaster John Durang left for America in 1789 and was the first emigrant dancing master, followed by Barney William, Dan O'Mahony and France X. Hennessy, who left Cork to 'join the great exodus in the 1840s to America' (Casey, 2006, pp. 417–8). They subsequently established Irish dancing schools in New York and Chicago to tutor second-generation Irish–Americans.

By the end of the nineteenth century Irish step dance and dancers were making a name for themselves in popular entertainment on the American stage. Mick Moloney (2002, p. 28) estimates that they were performing in vaudeville, minstrelsy and similar popular entertainments from the 1870s and identifies the strong presence of the Irish in most companies, who had performances of Irish dancers as well as Irish tenors and comedians. According to Moloney, Irish step dancing was a huge minstrel hit and immigrant Irish jig dancers like Jack Diamond became nationally known stars. Both Moloney and Hendrikson (1984) observe the preference for Irish jigs over the Scottish and English varieties.[1] Perhaps the most famous of the performers in the era of minstrelsy was William Henry Lane (aka Master Juba). Another well-known singer and dancer was Anthony Cannon (who changed his name to Tony Hart) in the 1870s and '80s. Fintan O'Toole (1997, p. 148) maintains there was 'an intimate connection between emigration and the survival of Irish dancing as an element of American popular culture'. To support his claim he refers to the fact that the father of Hollywood film actor Jimmy Cagney, Jerry Keohane, whose own father was the son of Famine emigrants, was a famous traditional Irish dancer who developed new versions of jigs and reels for the travelling variety show in which his son first appeared on stage and danced to Irish tunes played by renowned uilleann piper Patsy Touhey.

Early stage performances tended to construct negative stereotypes of the Irish and were characterised, according to Moloney (p. 29), by buffoonery and self-caricature. For instance, the character of the stage Irishman established at this time, deriving from British colonial representations, was portrayed as physically and mentally inferior, as 'apelike, ignorant, illiterate, credulous and superstitious; servile, debased and degraded – drunk and disorderly'. It was these representations that set the scene for the strong challenge to them by the Gaelic League in their own music and dance performances.

A number of writers point to the influence of Irish step dance on the evolution of American tap and of the early associations between Irish– and African–Americans. Carol Hendrikson (1984, p. 11) claims that 'it is mainly the Irish folk dance material picked up from the Irish labourers in the mines and on the railroads developed and adapted by the Blacks which supplies the core of the modern selection of tap dance steps'.

Terry Monaghan and Mo Dodson (2003, pp. 2–3) also attest to the 'the mutual cultural theft' that took place between these two communities at this time and ushered in the first forms of rhythm tap, frequently known as buck dancing. They refer to the conflicts between Master Juba and renowned dancer, John Diamond, and claim that the 'two-way character of this fusion was demonstrated by the profusion of professional clog, step and tap dancers of Irish origin in the following decades who appeared on minstrel and vaudeville stages and eventually in Hollywood and Broadway'.

Irish step dance had an influence not only on the developments of popular stage dance, as indicated above, but was also a source of inspiration for other dance forms. Isadora Duncan, the doyenne of modern dance in the USA, recalled how her own distinctive choreography was assembled from multiple sources, including Irish jigs. An extract from her memoir (quoted in Manning, 1993, p. 48) reads:

> I remember . . . my grandmother [dancing] Irish jigs: only I fancy that into these Irish jigs had crept some of Redskins – probably some of the gestures of the Redskins themselves, and, again, a bit of Yankee Doodle when Grandfather Colonel . . . came marching home from the Civil War. All this grandmother danced in the Irish jig; and I learnt it from her, and put into it my own aspiration of young America, and finally my great spiritual revelation of life from the lines of Walt Whitman. And that is the origin of the so-called Greek dance with which I have flooded the world.

Clearly, Irish dance influenced both popular and high-art dance forms in the USA and was in turn influenced by them, leading to innovation, creativity and the emergence of hybrid dance styles. This kind of cultural miscegenation, or more particularly the relative strength and direction of these influences, is the subject of ongoing debate amongst dance scholars.

Carby too believes that there was substantial interaction between the poor Irish and Africans in the ghettos of American cities (see Chapter Seven for more details). She draws on Charles Dickens' (1842, pp. 215–6, 218) description of a dancehall in Five Points, an Irish ghetto on New York's lower east side which Dickens visited in 1842, as evidence of the cultural contact between Irish–Americans and African–Americans. A similar scenario from the same ghetto is illustrated in a scene from Martin Scorsese's historically based film, *Gangs of New York*, in which an African–American character, accompanied by a fiddler, is doing a solo dance on the tavern stage. His performance, a mix of Irish and African–American styles, prompts a derisory comment from one of the main characters in the film, the notorious 'Bill the Butcher', about 'a jig dancing a jig'. Each of these accounts attests to the strength of interaction between these two marginalised and displaced ethnic groups in New York in the mid-nineteeth century.

Other scholars believe that the extent of interaction between Irish and African groups in urban life at that time is overplayed. Groneman (1978) challenges Grimes' interpretation of Dickens' American notes by suggesting that it is uncertain whether Dickens is describing an Irish dancehall or a black one. Natasha Casey (2002, p. 17) is also inclined to treat with caution reports of close alliances between the Irish and African–Americans, and points out that, while there are some well-documented instances of cordial relations between them, generally speaking 'Irish immigrants in the United States failed to establish alliances with African–American groups in the nineteenth century and little has altered since'.

Whatever the merit of each of these opposing viewpoints, there seems to be a general consensus that the Irish were eager to move out of the 'non-white' category (see Ignatiev, 1995) to which they had been assigned upon arrival in America and began to distance themselves from African–Americans at the earliest opportunity. In this regard there is ample documentation of the changing status of the Irish in American society and the rise of the respectable middle-class or 'lace-curtain' Irish (Ignatiev, 1995; Moloney, 2002; Rains, 2007). Dance in this context was used as a clear arbiter of social-class position and signified a rise in status. We see the exemplary figure of the respectable Irishman embodied in Francis O'Neill, a captain in the Chicago Police, who played a pivotal role in shaping the development of Irish music both in the USA and Ireland in the late nineteenth and early twentieth centuries. A member of the Chicago Music Club, he saw the Gaelic League as the means of keeping traditional Irish music and culture alive in America and gave it his wholehearted support (O'Connor, 1991, p. 80). O'Neill became involved in Irish musical activities and in collecting tunes and pub-lished the first collection of dance tunes as *The Dance Music of Ireland* in 1907.

The Gaelic League in the USA, of which O'Neill was a leading figure, was in O'Connor's view a 'self-consciously Irish movement devoted to the revival of Gaelic culture and a supporter of the Irish nationalist movement. It drew, for its support, on the better-off sections of Irish–American society, the emerging middle classes'. She reports that the League was very successful in this regard, with large attendances at the various functions and concerts held under its auspices. Through the organised functions of the League, a very formalised kind of group dancing emerged which was far removed from the country 'set' dances of Irish social life. The dances were more formal and took place in halls and hotels. It was also responsible for the development of céilí dancing, 'where long lines of dancers, girls on one side and boys on the other, faced each other, and danced steps to Irish jigs, reels and so on'. From O'Connor's account we can see a progressive formality developing in at least three ways: in the preferred dance forms, the venues chosen for dancing and the separation of the sexes on the dance floor.

O'Connor (p. 83) also observes that organisations like the League were interested in promoting Irish cultural events for a seated, middle-class, Irish–American audience. The attentive (silent) and seated (docile) audience was the ideal aspired to by the middle classes generally and was being progressively introduced into popular cultural performance (see Hansen, 2002, on cinema audiences in New York). There had been an organic connection between Irish music and dance as evidenced in the title of O'Neill's music collection. However, by the late 1880s, the distinction was being made between music for dancing and music for listening. By this time the members of the Chicago Music Club were interested in the music for itself and were happy to play for each other, without the presence of dancers.

The development of Irish music and dance at the beginning of the twentieth century in America is better documented than the earlier period under consideration, the latter providing accounts of well-known stage dancers as opposed to a social history of dance as a routine leisure activity. But despite the differences in data for the two periods, it seems clear that the development of dance was progressively reflecting the rise in social status of the Irish in American society and that dance continued to be a marker of both their ethnicity and changing status. The difference between the two eras might be viewed as a continuum, with the buffoonery and playfulness of the earlier period positioned at one end and the more tempered and sedate performance style of the later period at the other. However, changes in performance style appear to be a tendency only and seem to have varied between dance venues and performance contexts. Gedutis's (2004, p. 66) account of the dancehall context of the 1940s and 1950s, for instance, conveys a sense of play and where '[u]nself-conscious fun was the order of the day, and no one thought anything of the silly antics associated with dances to songs like "Shoe the donkey", a comical, almost childish song written to the tune of the classic mazurka "The Varsovienne"'. It is feasible then to suggest that tensions existed between the desire for respectability and formality associated with their upward social mobility on the one hand, and a desire for fun, vertigo and letting go on the other.

Irish Dance-Halls – A Taste of Home

Irish–American dancehalls became a feature of Irish–American life from 1900 onwards. According to Moloney (quoted in O'Connor, 1991, p. 83):

> [t]he dance hall in immigrant communities has always been a major social centre in America. It was the place where people recently arrived ... met people who were already there. Courtships took place there, it was a social centre ... and music and dancing were always interrelated there.

The advent of this kind of social dancing gave young men and women the freedom to select their own marriage partners as opposed to the 'old' world restrictions of family and community. These halls functioned in a variety of ways: enabling a change in the status of young people, acting as a social centre and enabling community building, and encouraging social and cultural continuity with home.

The dancehalls continued to enjoy popularity amongst the Irish and Irish–Americans well into the 1950s. Gedutis's (2004), finely grained ethnography of the five big Irish dancehalls in the Dudley Square area of Boston in the 1940s and 1950s attests to the close relationship between music and dance culture in Ireland and Boston during those decades. Historically a city of large Irish migration, economic circumstances in Ireland in these two decades led to a new wave of Irish emigrants arriving in the city. Her account provides a number of insightful observations about the complex process of identity construction through music and dance. The dancehalls operated at three levels: they brought people from 'home' together;

they provided a space in Boston for a tradition that was out of line with the Irish state's project of modernity; and they ensured a continuity of music and dance traditions among the next generation.

A number of Gedutis's respondents spoke of the relative appreciation of Irish music and dance in Boston in contrast to home, where, according to their accounts, it had been superceded by modern pop music. The years in which traditional music lay dormant in Ireland, she claims, were the very years in which the dancehalls thrived in Boston. In effect, the lively dancehalls in America played a critical role in preserving traditional music while it suffered a temporary decline in popularity in Ireland (p. 78). One of her respondents, Larry Reynolds, recalls having to carry his fiddle under his coat so he wouldn't be branded 'a "bog man", a "Mucker" – a country bumpkin . . . If people'd hear you playing traditional music, a jig or a reel, they'd sometimes be laughing at you' (p. 57). Many people confirmed that there was more Irish music in American dancehalls than at home, and some said that coming to Dudley Street for the first time was like taking a step back in time.

Despite traditional music's dormancy in Ireland, many people's interest was rekindled once they reached America because Irish music represented a taste of home. Asked if the 'Irishness' of the music was what drew them to the dancehalls, many would reply, 'No, It was just what I was used to' (p. 77), once again lending support to Connerton's claims about the importance of 'habit memory'. Rather than being drawn by the Irishness of the music, they were drawn to the social community that formed around the halls, says Joe Derrane. 'The music was familiar, maybe not their favourite, but it was familiar at least', he says. 'You had this common bond, and the meeting place. It was just the right place at the right time'. The familiarity with the music was echoed in dancers' desire for familiar people. When so far away from home, Irish emigrants sought out 'familiar faces, or at least people with familiar values, accents, and worldviews'. For the newly arrived from Ireland, it was a critical first stop. You might meet someone who would give you a dance. You might meet someone who could give you a job. 'If you visited the dance halls a few weeks in a row, you were *bound* to meet someone from your hometown' (p. 2). Gedutis (p. 77) believes that it was:

> The combination of the music and the social community that formed around it created the dance hall's magnetic atmosphere. Not too Irish, and yet just Irish enough – not the same as at home, but similar, foreign and yet familiar.

The interaction between recently arrived immigrants and Irish–Americans generated the immigrants' 'longing for what they had left behind' (p. 58). New immigrants were torn by dual desires; an eagerness for a new, modern life and a longing for the old, familiar one.

New immigrants lived in Irish neighbourhoods and dance promoters were obliged to cater to both the newly arrived as well as first- and second-generation Irish–Americans in order to run a successful dancehall. The most celebrated dancehall bands were the ones that specialised in both American and Irish music and performed on both traditional and modern instruments (p. 60). Dances included jigs and reels, perhaps a fling, interspersed with more modern dances such as waltzes, tangos and foxtrots. The eclectic mix of music and dance appealed to all the clientele (see fig. 18).

As for the Irish–Americans, they too lived in Irish neighbour-hoods, and their parents socialised almost exclusively with Irish people. On the one hand it was felt that first-generation Irish–Americans in the 1940s hung on to the 'Old Country' more tightly than the immigrants themselves. On the other there was a deep-seated sense of shame attached to being Irish. So while some migrants used dance to maintain a sense of ethnic identity and attachment to home, others used it to distance themselves from their social-class origins and/or ethnicity. Gene Frain, one of the dancers to whom Gedutis spoke, reported that her sister wouldn't dare go to Dudley Street, opting instead for the city's 'classier' nightclubs. As Frain herself put it, 'They were "upper crust Irish. Dudley Street wasn't high class at that point"' (p. 76).

Other writers attest to the conflicting feelings about practising traditional Irish culture in America. Mick Moloney (quoted in O'Connor, 1991, p. 86) observes that:

> There was a kind of ambivalence in their attitude to their culture: on the one hand they loved the dance hall, they loved the old music and they loved being Irish. On the other hand they wanted to shed the negative images coming from an oppressed peasant culture, and embedded in the culture itself was the dance music . . . They felt proud of their culture and . . . they felt ashamed. So

you found that even as the dance music was flourishing, at the same time it was going into a decline.

This same ambivalence towards traditional Irish culture is evident in the relative appeal of Irish step dance to first-generation Irish–Americans in cities like New York and Boston. Gedutis (p. 74) claims that, while many first-generation Irish–American children in the 1940s did learn step dancing, some of those concerned with 'getting ahead' avoided Irish music and dance altogether. Yu-Chen Lin (2010, p. 39) also reports a distaste for Irish dancing among Irish–American children at this time and that it was just about 'as interesting as going to the confession box'. If, in her opinion, 'the deep structure of the claim held by members of the diaspora on Irish dance was characterised by a longing for home, this longing was lost on the offspring of first-generation Irish emigrants' (p. 40). To support her claim she refers to Irish–American novelist Peter Quinn's account of American-born Irish children's reluctance to take dance lessons, based on his own experience of growing up in the Bronx in the 1950s. 'The joke', he is quoted as saying, 'was the kids who took Irish dancing lessons were the ones who couldn't run faster than their parents' (p. 39). Rather than being based on Irish–Americans' appreciation of traditional Irish culture, Yu-Chen Lin argues that the longing for home that was most commonly thought to originate in Irish–American communities was actually coming from the Irish tourism sector, and that it was induced by 'supplying a cultural memory that is most likely not there, in order to induce the return of their offspring as tourists (p. 40). She supports her argument by drawing on Stephanie Rains' (2007) analysis of Bord Fáilte travelogues from this time. Rains sees these films as mobilising a diasporic memory of Ireland as home for second-generation Irish, and a trip to Ireland is represented as a form of return home. Yu-Chen Lin's account, unlike Rains', fails to acknowledge the dialectical relationship that exists between tourist imagery and collective memory, and which informs the multiple and at times contradictory images of home that circulate in popular culture (see Leonard below for further discussion of how cultural memories of home, some of which are sourced in tourist imagery, may, in fact, promote traditional music and dance practice in contemporary Britain). Whatever the extent of the reluctance by first- and second-generation Irish-Americans to learn Irish step dancing, evidently there was sufficient interest among sufficient numbers to form a critical mass and to ensure not only its survival in America but thriving into the twenty-first century.

Bringing it all Back Home – Dancing Schools, Feiseanna and 'The Worlds'

The dance schools which had been established by first-generation migrants fulfilled a number of important functions for second-generation Irish–Americans. As already witnessed in other dance performance contexts, one of the primary functions of dance classes was to cement the connection with home through the inter-generational continuity of dance practice. A second was to position themselves in relation to other groups. Drawing on Kenny (2000, pp. 71, 106–8) and Miller's (1985, pp. 248, 319–20) work, Yu-Chen Lin (p. 39) points to the positive function of dance classes for Irish emigrants. At a time, she writes:

> when Irish immigrants suffered from racial discrimination and harsh competition with their counterparts from other cultures, these dancing schools offered an opportunity to make connections with home, if not an alternative to alcoholism, racial politics and gang violence to steer away from mental problems that had plagued many first-generation Irish Americans.

The dance schools fed into competitive Irish step dance organised around feiseanna. The biggest strongholds for feiseanna outside of Ireland were places where the Irish had emigrated in large numbers, including Britain, the USA, Australia, Canada and New Zealand. They were organised by the Irish Dancing Commision (Comisiún le Rincí Gaelacha) in each country. About 200 feiseanna are held in North America annually and these are, in Cullinane's (1997, p. 199) view, very much family-oriented affairs and social occasions for the Irish community abroad. While the dancing is the dominant feature they include other aspects of Irish culture. Irish sporting events appeal more to the boys and men, while the girls and young women become involved more in the dancing competitions. It is very much a family day and there is something for each member of the family, young or old, male or female.

The national dance championships expanded to a global level with the establishment of the World Irish Dancing Championship, commonly known as 'The Worlds', in 1970. Held annually, the competition draws dancers from a number of countries who, as it were, bring Irish dance back home and create a permanent network of the Irish diaspora through dance (see Cullinane, 1997; Jessica Tomell-Presto, 2003; Wulff, 2005). We learn from Cullinane (1997, p. 194) that some 15,000 Irish dancers from New Zealand to Australia, North America, England, Scotland and Ireland compete annually in their own area to represent their region at the championships. About 2,500 finalists participate in this eight-day event, one of the biggest cultural events of its kind in the world. For many of these visitors their participation often constitutes their first visit to Ireland, the home of their ancestors, but for the accompanying parents and teachers it has become part of the annual visit 'home'.[2]

While the accounts above confirm the role of feiseanna in creating a sense of attachment to community values, the competitive nature of the dancing raises questions about their role in promoting individualist values as opposed to collective ethnic ones. Cullinane, who has himself been an adjudicator with CLRG for many years, believes that it is the love of competition rather than a true appreciation of their heritage that motivates North American dancers to travel several thousand miles per year. Casey (2002, p. 13) also maintains that there is a connection between the ideologies of Irish folk dance and the values of individuality associated with the American Dream (the issue of individual identity and a sense of Irishness will be addressed further in Chapter Seven). However, it seems that the values of the collective as expressed in the community identity-building function and individual competitive values such as those expressed in a desire to win 'The Worlds' are not mutually exclusive but rather appear to operate in tandem in most of the dance contexts considered in this chapter.

The discussion so far has centred on dance in the USA and I would now like to draw on accounts of dance among the Irish diaspora elsewhere. This Cook's tour should not suggest that the experience of the diaspora is similar in each location, but, while acknowledging the differences and complexities of diasporic life and experience, I do want to make the point that dance has functioned to create and maintain Irish ethnic identity in each of the selected locations.

From the early days of the Gaelic League, as witnessed in Chapter Two, the leading figures of the London branch were predominantly middle-class, with careers and reputations at stake, and with a vested interest in the reputation of the Irish in Britain. It will be recalled that the London branch of the League was the first to promote 'properly conducted' Irish social evenings based on the format of the Scottish evenings being held in London in the 1890s. The first, as noted earlier, was held in Bloomsbury Hall, located in an area that could be regarded as the cultural centre of the capital city and a venue familiar to a middle- and upper-class clientele. Cullinane (p. 197) observes how the League was extremely conscious of the rowdy image of the Irish created by other events held in London and figure dance being more refined than sets or quadrilles. The latter 'were performed without any prescribed footwork and a degree of frivolity and excessive enjoyment which led the League to fear that this might reflect badly on the Irish'.

Bloomsbury Hall proved to be the exception to the rule as a venue for Irish dance in London but it continued to thrive throughout the twentieth century in pubs, clubs and dancehalls located in almost exclusively Irish communities. Reg Hall (1994, p. 297), who has extensively researched music and dancing among the Irish in London, reports that Irish dance in Britain during the 1950s and 1960s was both a badge of respectability and a means of creating and maintaining a weak version of a nationalist identity:

> The iconography of Irish Dance was still nationalist, but until the Troubles flared up in 1969, nationalism for the parents of Irish dancers was more to do with personal and group identity and solidarity than with a political ideology.

Immigrant mothers could involve themselves in Irish dance through their children. It was a respectable Roman Catholic activity and provided an alternative to their husbands' less respectable public-house culture. Cullinane (p. 200) too notes the predominantly female nature of the feiseanna, as sitting indoors in a hall did not appeal to the men. Dancing was not allowed in most of the Irish pubs in London although '[o]ccasionally the sign forbidding dancing was ignored and a tiny space was cleared for someone to shuffle, or step a reel or a hornpipe' (Hall, p. 320). In addition, Hall notes (p. 351) that music making in London lost its function as an accompaniment to domestic dancing and as a consequence took on an entertainment function as listening music. The first effect was the loss of specific tunes for old-fashioned step dances, sets and couple dances. Thus polkas, hop jigs, single jigs, schottishes, flings and waltzes were never (or only rarely) played in pubs or Comhaltas meetings. There was some notion, he suggests, that they were second-class material, unworthy of being played in public, although many older musicians still felt an affection for those tunes they knew in their youth, and musicians who would not normally play waltzes in pubs or Comhaltas might play any number at a wedding reception. Julia and John Clifford, who in more recent times have been fêted for their large repertoire of slides and polkas, had almost given them up as old-fashioned and redundant by the mid-1950s.

The dancehall was the most popular venue for dancing in London and, according to Hall, the most popular dances were the old-time waltz and the Siege of Ennis, sets and half-sets being included in the programmes at the *Galtymore* in Cricklewood and Quex Road, dancehalls with an almost exclusively Irish clientele. It seems that men were less inclined to dance to modern tunes and took refuge in adjacent pubs during the 'prolonged stretches of modern dancing' (p. 318). Irish songs were among the most popular at dances during the 1950s and early 1960s, such as Bridie Gallagher's songs and older ones like 'The Old Bog Road' and 'Boolavogue' (p. 297). These songs might be sung by a band vocalist and couples sang along to the music as they danced. Here we see another example of Connerton's 'incorporating practice' through a combination of body movement and voice of an imagined homeland, or a specific place within it such as Boolavogue.

Dance, Authenticity and Cultural Memory

Fifty years on from the dancers of the 1950s, Marion Leonard's (2005, p. 516) research on music and dance conducted in the Irish communities of Coventry and Liverpool confirms how British-born second- and third-generation Irish use music and dance 'in the construction of personal identities and also in the production and maintenance of social bonds and interactions'. Her work confirms that music and dance continued to be a powerful source of cultural memory and a signifier of ethnic belonging for the hyphenated Irish in the latter part of the twentieth century. Her research was based on one-to-one interviews with the Liverpool Irish (11 participants aged between 13 and 70 years old), who strongly identified themselves as second- or third-generation Irish and were actively involved in Irish music and dance groups. The comments of music and dance practitioners 'revealed how value was placed on the sensuous act of the body in movement and on the function of performance as a public articulation of Irishness' (p. 516). The link between cultural traditions and personal identity was often naturalised in the language people used. A number of people expressed their connection with traditional music and dance using metaphors related to the body. One dancer joked that it was like a contagion: 'It is like a disease, you never get rid of it! There doesn't seem to be any cure for it.' The children in Coventry commented that the music has the power to alter their emotional state and a number described the corporeal effect of the sound in making them want to dance (p. 524). Leonard explains this powerful emotional impact by drawing on de Nora's observation that music is a 'powerful *aide-memoire*', not just because of its 'co-presence with other things – people, events, scenes' (2000, p. 66) but also because music unfolds over time and so can aid the recollection of a particular space or moment:

> music and dance performance was a physical demonstration or embodiment of identity, operating as a public signal of identification as Irish. The body was being put to work in articulating a connection with an imagined 'home'. (519)

Leonard identifies a second function of music and dance amongst the participants: the opportunity they provided for people of different generations to interact and facilitate the continuance of community activities (p. 516). Music and dance practices were valued 'not just for reasons of tradition, aesthetics or personal involvement but as *a means with which to share social interaction* with others of Irish background' (p. 516). Liverpool interviewees 'articulated a double sense of belonging both to a home of past ancestors and to a local community within Liverpool founded upon a shared ethnic identity' (p. 522).

Music and dance are frequently used to construct a sense of home in terms of geographic location and landscape. Boundary maintenance is part of this process and ethnomusicologist Martin Stokes (1994, p. 6) claims that 'music is used by social actors in specific local situations to erect boundaries, to maintain distinctions between us and them, and how terms such as "authenticity" are used to justify these boundaries' (see also O'Shea, 2008, for a comparative study of

Irish music in Australia and Ireland). Leonard's participants also used Irish music and dance to invoke a connection with Ireland that was both imagined and a badge of authenticity. Some of the responses tied the music back to the physical landscape and particular places in Ireland. The homeland imagined by the participants was composed of a bricolage of images and texts that surrounded them in their everyday lives – television programmes, magazines, advertisements, postcards, mythic images and so on. It was also based on their memories of summer holidays spent in Ireland. Participants' comments indicated that the music had the capacity to 'resonate with multiple, even, conflicting, productions of Irishness' (p. 527).

Irish dance in Britian appears to be broadly similar in terms of its role in ethnic identity formation to that in the USA: as a way of enacting respectability and of achieving status in their host countries, as well as a way of connecting to home. Strict comparison is not possible because some of the accounts reviewed above relate to a variety of dance forms, institutional contexts and time periods. There is possibly one major difference between the two: Irish dance became a more integral part of American public culture in contrast to Britain where it was more hidden within exclusively Irish communities.[3] The relative visibility of the Irish in America and Britain has historical roots, and, while there may have been racial prejudice and discrimination towards the Irish in America, it did not have the same effect as the long historical colonial relationship with Britain had on the Irish in Britain.

As in Liverpool and Coventry, cultural memory is also a powerful force in the Irish step-dance community in Newfoundland. Following Toelken's (2003) idea that 'the expressive arts may become more significant on the periphery, becoming a signifier of not just the land that was left, but the people, customs and way of life that some may try to preserve in their new homes', dance scholar Kristin Harris Walsh (2008, p. 127) claims that 'Irishness' has flourished in Newfoundland and Labrador through the arts generally and through dance in particular. Harris Walsh identifies three main types of step dancing in the province: traditional Newfoundland step dance, Irish–Newfoundland step dance and traditional Irish step dance. For her, the crucial element in explaining the vibrancy of Irish dance in Newfoundland is the cultural memory of Newfoundland as Irish. Despite the fact that the Irish are neither the largest ethnic group nor the predominant settlers in the province, Irish culture tends to dominate because of the mobilisation of collective memory and the continuous perception of a strong cultural link to Ireland. And it is the perceived cultural link to Ireland that, to a large extent, informs Newfoundland's identity.

The main proponents of the Irish–Newfoundland dancers are the St Pat's dancers', a children's step-dance group based in St Johns. Founded by the Christian Brother Samuel Murphy in the 1930s, it comprised five boys from the St Patrick's school. Brother Max Murray brought dances from New York in the 1940s, broadening the repertoire of the group and furthering their dance knowledge. Interestingly he had studied with Fred Astaire and Ginger Rogers and 'brought a flair for performance along with dances learned in the American-Irish communities in New York' (p. 130). The fate of Irish step dance waxed and waned with the 1930s, '70s and '90s (the latter due to the influence of *Riverdance*), marked as periods of revival. Francie Gow, the fiddle player for St Pat's Dancers in 1997, thought that *Riverdance* brought step dancing into the popular realm; 'it has not only brought it into the forefront of global consciousness, it has made it appealing to watch, to practise and to perform'. Because of this, Gow believes that 'there is a renewed interest in the more traditional forms of step dance, thereby merging the vernacular and the popular and allowing both to exist comfortably within the same cultural space' (quoted in Harris-Walsh, pp. 127–28)'. According to Harris Walsh, a feeling of pride in the dance is instilled in the children, enabling the collective memory of Newfoundland's Irish heritage to continue in both the dancer and the public they entertain. The hybridity of the dancing facilitates children to teach each other, to choreograph new pieces and to set them to local tunes. In this context the cultural background of the individual dancer is irrelevant. It is rather the cultural memory of Newfoundland as Irish and the dance style's Irish roots that are of primary importance. This is, in Harris Walsh's view, what enables the St Pat's Dancers to continue to be a prevalent force in the folk arts community and give them prominence in Newfoundland culture.

Here and There: Between Hybridity and Authenticity

Whether performed in Britain, North America or elsewhere, whether at house parties or in dancehalls, school halls, pubs or stage, whether outdoors or indoors, whether competitively or non-competitively, whether children or adult, dance, as we have seen, was an integral part of the social life of the Irish diaspora throughout the twentieth century. Weaving its way through an eclectic mix of forms, meanings and institutional contexts, it played a key role in the maintenance of Irish ethnic identity. The experience of migration also generated a strong desire for community building in the host country and the transmission of Irish dance from one generation to the next as well as a desire to connect with the home country.

However, the close relationship between dance and ethnic identity does not mean that it can be either essentialised or reified. It may be regarded more accurately as 'a cultural site in which the . . . migrants spatially inscribe their experience, using their bodies as a means of communication' and where dance is 'continuously recreated by the agents (i.e. dancers and spectators) who are involved in its enactment under the changing conditions of the context in which they are located' (Tabar, 2005, p. 155). We saw how these changing conditions affected the shape and meanings of Irish dance in diverse circumstances. Its performance on the American stage was instrumental in constructing stereotypes of the Irish both positive and negative in American public culture. In some periods Irish emigrants interacted with other ethnic and cultural groups to develop genres such as American tap, vaudeville and modern dance, while in others they erected boundaries between groups leading to the decline in the mixing of dance forms between ethnic groups. We also saw how the search for respectability led to a disengagement with the rowdier and more *déclassé* aspects of Irish dance culture, as evidenced in the Gaelic League and in the avoidance of Irish dancehalls in Boston in the 1940s and 1950s. Both of these moves can be seen to reflect the changing social-class position of the Irish in the early and mid-twentieth century.

Irish dance meant different things to emigrants: for some it displayed a pride in Irish identity; others expressed an ambivalence towards it, and others still distanced themselves from it. Even the term 'Irish' when applied to dancing had different meanings. For some it was confined to a dance form that was seen to be authentically Irish, such as Irish step dance. For others it was a mix of Irish and other influences to produce a hybrid dance form, as in Newfoundland. For others still, Irish dance was associated with the venues where Irish musicians played, or indeed dancing in a location where the majority of the dancers were from Ireland.

Migrant journeys, as we have seen, brought Irish dance to the cities of Britain, North America and Australia throughout the twentieth century. It is towards the end of that century that we see a return journey to the homeland and the start of yet another global journey in the form of *Riverdance*. Not only did this new incarnation of Irish step dance narrate the story of Irish emigration to America but the two principal dancers in the original show, Michael Flatley and Jean Butler, were themselves Irish–American. It is to this journey that we now turn to explore a new era in the globalisation of Irish dance.

CHAPTER SEVEN

The Riverdance *Effect*
Culture Industries and Global Irishness

> So I think if you're going to show Irishness you've got to . . . it's
> almost like the step change that Riverdance made for Irish
> dancing, and that's often used as an analogy in our business. That
> Irish dancing was girls with ringlets, not sexy, red hair, don't want
> to do it [laughs], not cool . . . and suddenly you have Jean Butler
> – stunning-looking girl, fantastically fit, brilliantly energetic, and
> amazing music and you think, God, like it went from there to
> there overnight. So you know, it completely changed what people
> thought of Ireland, so it's almost like in a way you've got to do
> Riverdance if you want to do Irishness.

These are the words of a managing director of an Irish advertising
agency describing the mandatory inclusion of *Riverdance* in updating
the branding of Irishness (quoted in O'Boyle, 2011, p. 176). The
show that had begun life as a seven-minute interval act in the
Eurovision Song Contest of 1994 was by the end of the decade
weaving its way across the global stage and, as witnessed in the quote
above, was becoming a 'master signifier' (Coulter and Coleman,
2003, p. 4) of Irish identity. Its mesmeric rise to fame is by now well
rehearsed: how the electric interval performance brought the studio
audience to their feet in a prolonged standing ovation thus attracting
a viewing audience it could never hope for in other circumstances –
three hundred million viewers, wordwide (Smyth, 1996, p.33); and
how it received such popular and critical acclaim that the show's
producer, Moya Doherty, with her partner John McColgan, decided
to form the company Tyrone Productions to produce a full two-
hour music and dance show based on the act (see figs 19 and 20). At
the height of its fame the show had four travelling dance troupes,

making Irish dance once again at least as popular and fashionable as it was at the beginning of the century, and this time not just with a national audience but a global one. And it was more than a music and dance show; it was an extremely successful product of the Irish cultural industries, with a variety of spin-off products such as videos, DVDs and CDs. In essence, it was one of the most successful ventures in Irish cultural production of the twentieth century.

Because of its phenomenal success, *Riverdance* significantly influenced the popularity of Irish step dance in Ireland and elsewhere. Michael Flatley, the lead dancer with the original show, went on to produce a series of his own shows, including *Lord of the Dance* and *Feet of Flame*. It spawned a number of other dance troupes who also played to national and international audiences. Step dancers became *de rigueur* in the line-up for entertainment shows for the tourist market (see fig. 21). Step dance enjoyed an increased visibility on Irish television too, as in the reality show *Celebrity Jigs and Reels*; as the title implies, this was a step-dance competition between celebrities (but danced to non-traditional music) made for RTÉ. The winners of the first series of the *All-Ireland Talent Show* in 2009 were young sean-nós dancers from Connemara, the sean-nós style itself having enjoyed a comeback post-*Riverdance*. This era also saw a surge of interest in step-dance classes both in Ireland and abroad (e.g. see Masero, 2010). Overall, the status of Irish step dance had risen considerably, from the era of competitions on the backs of lorries to performances in Radio City Music Hall, and with the prospect of 'global glamour' (Coutas, 2006) for the best dancers.

As suggested in the introductory chapter, *Riverdance,* as a key cultural marker of Irishness at the close of the twentieth century, might be usefully book-ended with the role of the céilí at the beginning. Their juxtaposition begs the question of whether the meanings of Irishness as constituted through dance might have changed over the course of the century. And a related question follows: what might the structure, narrative and performance context of *Riverdance* imply about Irish cultural identity in a contemporary context? In this chapter I hope to address these questions by drawing on two bodies of evidence.[1] The first is an overview of selected literature that engages with the production and consumption context of *Riverdance*. The second is based on conversations with a number of young dancers who performed in a post-*Riverdance* show in a

Dublin pub/hotel venue in the summer of 2000. The analysis of the critical literature (textual analysis) reveals some of the meanings of Irishness attached to the show. Conversations with dancers give an insight into the meanings they build around the shows and into the ways they negotiate their personal identities in relation to *Riverdance*-style performance. The findings from these accounts reveal the diverse, and at times contradictory, meanings of Irishness as danced in an era of cultural globalisation.

Riverdance, Identity and Cultural Globalisation

Riverdance is commonly regarded as the paramount exemplar of the current phase of the globalisation of Irish dance. This process is not a recent one but, as evidenced in previous chapters, it has been global or, at least, 'proto-global' over hundreds of years (Kavanagh et al., 2008) in the sense that it was continuously influenced by music and dance styles from elsewhere. Two examples of this globality referred to in previous chapters are the introduction of set dances from Europe in the early eighteenth century and North American influences on competitve step dance reflected in the introduction of the World Championships in 1970. However, in the contemporary period, globalising forces are not only intensified but are also qualitatively different from what went before. Three different stages of step-dance evolution in Ireland have been identified by a number of writers (O'Connor, 1998; Foley, 2001; Kavanagh et al., 2008) and these can be categorised broadly as local, national and global. The local context was one in which dance was performed as an integral part of the entertainment rituals of everyday life. This was followed by the national era, in which step dance was organised around the competitive system of the feiseanna. Finally, the contemporary global era is characterised by an international hybrid style performed for theatre shows and based on a commercial entertainment model. So if we look historically at the production context of Irish step dance, we can say that it has been transformed from a substantially amateur and voluntary leisure activity to a professional and commercial enterprise.[2] Dance can now be seen as a commodity within a global entertainment industry in which performances are increasingly driven and shaped by economic imperatives. What are the effects of the globalisation process on step dance? Before attempting to answer this question it is necessary to ask a prior one about the meaning of cultural globalisation itself.

While the concept of cultural globalisation is a protean one and there are diverse views on its effects, approaches to it can be usefully placed within three broad categories with regard to their impact on local/national cultural values and practices. Scholars such as Wallerstein (1991) and Schiller (1976) view the relationship between national and global cultures as one of mutual opposition and the consequences of globalisation as negative. They hold the view that traditional cultures are continuously eroded by an onslaught of mass-produced entertainment, thus creating a cultural homogeneity. More recently, Morley and Robins (1995), while not subscribing to the valorisation of local cultures, nonetheless see globalisation as utilising traditional local cultures for profit in the global marketplace. Cultural globalisation, in their view, is a process in which cultural products from all over the world are taken and transformed into commodities to be sold in the cosmopolitan marketplace. There is an acknowledgement too that the process of globalisation is a complex one and that the tensions and contradictions attendant on it can be both positive and negative. Robertson (1995) depicts a situation in which local/traditional cultures are interwined with the global in a process called 'glocalisation'. Tomlinson (1999, p. 20) is also aware of the 'complex connectivity' of globalisation and believes the most pertinent questions to pose are not those about the exchange of global cultural commodities *per se* but how the process:

> alters the context of meaning construction: how it affects people's sense of identity, the experience of place and of the self in relation to place, how it impacts on the shared understandings, values, desires, myths, hopes and fears that have developed around locally situated life.

Albeit in a much more limited and focused way, these are the questions addressed here in relation to the effects of *Riverdance.*

If we consider the appeal of the Spanish dance show [*Cibayí* (1992)] with lead dancer Joaquín Cortés, around the same time as *Riverdance,* television progammes such as *Strictly Come Dancing* or the use of dancing bodies in television advertisements, we realise that movement and dance are now key to the success of global entertainment culture.[3] The emphasis on movement in popular entertainment can be seen as a reflection of the ways in which the mobile body, cultural identities and globalising processes are increasingly interlinked. A number of writers have pointed to an increasing emphasis on the moving body in the formation of personal identities in contemporary Western societies. Appadurai (1996) sees contemporary life in terms of global 'flows' characterised by the mobility of people, goods, money and ideas across the world. The body itself has become a key signifier of identity in the contemporary Western world (see Featherstone et al., 1991). Embodied performance in contemporary popular culture is also a vehicle for communicating identity. In this regard Tim Edensor (2002, p. 72) notes that 'particular kinds of performance are intended to draw attention to the self, are a vehicle for transmitting identity, and others are decoded by others as denoting identity irrespective of the actor's intentions'. (Both of these constructions of identity – the decoding by others (critics) and self-decoding (dancers) – will be explored in the discussion of *Riverdance* below.) It is plausible to suggest, therefore, that at least part of *Riverdance*'s appeal can be attributed to the increase in global mobility and representations of the moving body in popular global entertainment during the 1990s. However, there are also culturally/nationally specific influences on the production of *Riverdance* that need to be considered in any attempt to understand its role in the globalisation process.

Choreographing the Celtic Tiger

Riverdance is very closely associated with the Celtic Tiger due to the fact that the first two-hour show performed in the Point Depot in Dublin in 1995 was co-terminous with the Irish economy emerging from the recession of the 1980s. From the mid-1990s Ireland was beginning to experience what for some was an economic boom which lasted for approximately fifteen years. One might say that the Celtic Tiger marked the apotheosis of a 'successful' globalised Irish economy before its collapse in 2007. The economic growth witnessed during this period was in no small measure fuelled by cultural production, including music and dance. This is evidenced in the international success of bands such as U2, the Corrs, the Cranberries, and Celtic new age singers such as Enya (see Cronin and O'Connor, 2000, p. 177; Rains, 2007, p. 13). The success of *Riverdance* marked the beginning of this new era for Irish dance. Donncha Kavanagh, Carmen Kuhling and Kieran Keohane (2008) see *Riverdance* as a paradigmatic exemplar of the correspondence between the globalisation of Irish culture and of the Irish economy more broadly. They suggest that this correspondence can be interpreted in opposing ways: that postmodernists and liberals would see it as 'an illustration of the creativity that drives and is produced by the cultural economy', whereas critical theorists would perceive it as an impoverishment of culture that is inherent in the globalising process of late capitalism.

Using a Weberian interpretivist approach, Kavanagh, Kuhling and Keohane see *Riverdance* as part of a *Zeitgeist*, 'a spirit that unites seemingly disparate and unrelated forms of action – economic and cultural – in terms of the affinities between them'. Such phenomena – dance in this instance – express the *Zeitgeist*, the unifying 'spirit of the times' (p. 728). According to the authors, *Riverdance* parallels the transformation of working relations in Ireland in the nineteenth and twentieth centuries. They trace the relationship between work and dance in the three eras of Irish dance development and maintain that it is characterised by a gradual and progressive 'refinement' from the local, through the national, and into the global phase. In the traditional/local community work and dance were organised as constituent elements of a unified whole. It then moved through a modern rational differentiation of the spheres of work and aesthetics in which the realms of 'work' and 'dance' were constituted as separate and even opposed activities that are recombined and unified through state-approved 'invented tradition' and the organising practices of modern national society. The current phase represented by *Riverdance* is one wherein dance, which had previously been confined to the world of leisure and popular recreation, becomes highly specialised professional work. The latter the authors refer to as 'workdance', which is organised as a simulacrum of 'tradition' (p. 729).

Riverdance, they argue, is 'purported to be a postmodern phenomenon, an aesthetic representation of the creative culture of globalisation'. They see this as in line with the promises of global neo-liberalism to transcend the limitations of global capitalism as a mode of production. Not only does it promise the 'liberation' of market forces, but equally the 'promotion' of entrepreneurship and innovation. They point to Moya Doherty's account of the creation of *Riverdance* as expressing this kind of liberation and mobility. They also see it expressed in O'Toole's (2003, p. 153) claim that what made *Riverdance* more than another creative product was 'the way it liberated locked-up elements of Irish tradition, the way it became, quite self-consciously, a parable of the modernisation of Irish culture'. However, the authors see a problem with the idea that *Riverdance* is the locus of such liberation, creativity and innovation, as is claimed. There is a massive contradiction between the representation of *Riverdance* as a postmodern phenomenon when it is, in their view, a decidedly modern one. It is so because, while dancers' bodies appear to be liberated and eroticised, they are, in fact, 'disciplined bodies, subjectified, transformed, improved and put to work as surely as the bodies of the patient, the prisoner or the proletariat forensically described by Foucault'. Riverdancers, they argue, are 'work dancers, cut from a pattern, rigorously quality controlled' (p. 738). Consequently *Riverdance* is for them a site of one the main myths of global capitalism.

Kavanagh et al.'s analysis of *Riverdance* as a modern phenomenon echoes the mass-culture debates of the 1920s and 1930s in which dance was seen as a reflection of the machine of industrial capitalism. It is particularly reminiscent of Kracauer's (1995 [1927]) writing on dancing bodies as 'mass ornament' in which he perceived the abstractness and precision of the movement of dancers in popular stage shows of the time, such as *The Tiller Girls*, reflecting the rationalising process of the capitalist system. Andre Levinson (1991 [1928]) writing at the same time draws a similar conclusion when he comments on the 'meaninglessness of their precise, abstract, machine-like choreography'. The dancers' movements are seen in both cases as an expression of the logic of mass production through the precision of their dancing.[4] The fashion for precise synchronised movement was also visible in other areas of popular culture, such as stadia sports displays and gymnastics, during these decades (see Burt, 1998). Perhaps one of the best-known examples is provided in the mass spectacle of the synchronised movement of bodies at the Olympic Games of 1936, signifying the power of Germany united under Hitler and captured in Leni Riefenstahl's film of the event.

For Kavanagh et al. the contradictions inherent in the representations of *Riverdance* are very much part of a wider contradiction, or con trick, within global capitalism, which is that traditional culture is taken, repackaged and sold back to the original owners of that culture. Far from representing a cultural renaissance, the authors claim, the emergence of a rejuvenated spirit of creative enterprise animating new forms of global organisation and work as exemplified in *Riverdance* may in fact be 'an Irish wake – exuberant, but as a defence against death' (p. 739). Given the bleak state of the Irish economy by 2008, their analysis may have been prescient.

While Kavanagh et al.'s account is for the most part a trenchant critique of *Riverdance* as part of a global neo-liberal cultural economy, they don't dismiss it entirely. Rather they believe that a tension exists in the history of Irish dance (and, indeed, in Irish culture in general) between the expression of dominant accounts and of counter-discourses which provide a potential for creativity and innovation in both economy and culture. *Riverdance* and its derivatives provide interesting contemporary manifestations of these tensions, one example being Michael Flatley's show *Celtic Tiger*, which, in their view, 'draws deeply on the oppositional discourses of traditional Irish nationalism'. Ultimately, though, they conclude that 'these dance shows are icons of, and embedded in, a late-capitalist system where "Irishness" is but a commodified sign traded in a global "alterity industry"' (Huggan, quoted in Kavanagh et al., 2008, p. 739).

Sherlock's (1999) analysis of *Riverdance* also sees it as deeply embedded in global capitalism. She argues that shows such as *Riverdance* may be diversions from the realities of globalisation, while conceding that it may have a positive role in terms of its meanings and pleasures for the Irish diaspora. She goes on to warn readers (again, in a Frankfurt School kind of critique of mass culture) of the possibility that:

> Although *Riverdance* is uplifting, and may offer a celebration of a good way of life to some, we should also be sceptical of the extent to which popular forms are valued products of cultural groups, and how their resonances may be nostalgic diversions from the real struggles in consumer capitalism and dance of all kinds. (p. 217)

Sherlock acknowledges that in the reality of the 1990s 'all forms of dance have to respond to the dictates of financial and cultural constraints'. However, we should not forget that *Riverdance* as a cultural commodity 'is serving the interests of capitalist profit-making' (p. 205). Though the logic of the market and the profit motive are mentioned by Sherlock, they are treated in a fairly abstract way.[5] Her critique does address a couple of specific aspects of the production of *Riverdance* that she believes are affected by global capitalism. One is the operation of a 'creative ideology' at work in a number of areas: in the modernising of ideas of traditional styles, in the 'artistic intentions of using themes and symbols, and in the levelling international style' (p. 214). The technical prowess of *Riverdance* is also germane to its function within global capitalism. She posits that possession of 'modern technological knowledge is the primary requirement of being able to advance in the western version of the "good life". Technical brilliance is no less important in dance than it is in any other branch of the market-place' (p. 214). She sees Riverdancers' 'levelling up to unbelievable technical prowess, to incredible professional showmanship' as being a crucial element in encouraging other subordinate cultural groups to become 'modernised, disciplined and corporate and able to partake fully in industrialised labour'. Although she does not explain the specific context in which she refers to the Irish as a subordinate cultural group, her argument about the importance of technology in creative production is a persuasive one. *Riverdance* is a highly technologised production. Not only are the technical elements of sound and lighting produced to 'world-class' standards, but dancers' bodies are technologised in a number of ways, such as the placing of microphones in the dancers' shoes to increase the percussion sound and to give a hyper-real effect to the footwork. The dancer's bodies are also technologised, in the sense that, as suggested by Kavanagh et al., there is a blurring of boundaries between human and machine.[6]

Narratives of Irishness

The storyline of *Riverdance* is a simple one in the classic narrative tradition: a beginning, where people live in harmony with nature in their native land; a middle stage of dis-equilibrium, where the balance of life is disturbed and the Irish are forced into exile; followed by an end (and the promise of a new beginning) in their new land. While Kavanagh et al. and Sherlock's critiques focus more on dance style and production values, other analysts place more emphasis on the *Riverdance* narrative. To consider this perspective more fully I draw substantially on Carby (2001) because she offers a scholarly critique from both a feminist and African–American studies perspective. The latter position enables her to offer a unique perspective on the racial dimensions which she sees operative in the New York *Riverdance* show as well as in Michael Flatley's subsequent show, *Lord of the Dance*.

Her general objective is to examine how Irishness is constructed within these shows. The cultural and aesthetic politics of *Riverdance*, she claims, imagine and present Irishness for global consumption as the story of the Irish as one successful ethnic group among many others. *Riverdance* is set within the frame of multiculturalism, which in her view presents:

> a global culture without history . . . [that] affirms the importance of national cultural boundaries in the face of their combination into large, corporate controlled, political and economic international entities, like the new Europe, while at the same time denying the internationalisation of its peoples and cultures whose actual histories have been messily intertwined in social, political and economic relations that consistently crossed and recrossed racial and ethnic boundaries and which are embodied in miscegenated cultural forms rather than ethnically pure folk cultures. (p. 330)

The representation of each of the ethnic groups in the New York show as discrete and pure cultures, she claims, is historically inaccurate. To support her argument she draws on contemporaneous accounts by writers such as Charles Dickens of the everyday lives of African–American and Irish cultures in places like the Five Points in New York city in the 1860s. These accounts attest to the fact that Irish and African–Americans lived, worked, copulated, cohabited and danced together in the local taverns. This close proximity allowed for a mutual exchange of dance steps, and provided an opportunity for learning from each other. She also acknowledges that:

> any search for the purely Africanist roots of American dance must also pay attention to this moment (miscegenation), a moment in which what becomes known now as a pre-eminently black dance form is developed from the black adoption, adaptation and transformation of the Irish jig. The roots and routes of black and Irish cultural migrations coalesce and reform in these basements. (p. 346)

The miscegenation that Carby refers to was confined to the lower classes. Indeed, she indicates that the respectable classes of the time were outraged at this and continuously called for action to 'discipline and control the mingling of bodies and cultures' (p. 347). This is the kind of cultural interchange between Irish and African–Americans in the nineteenth century that Carby sees as totally obliterated from *Riverdance*, despite the fact that African–Americans are represented in the show in the form of the Gospel choir.

The claim to ethnic purity is clearly illustrated in the precision tap chorus line of *Riverdance*. According to Carby, this particular piece of choreography was developed for the chorus line of *Chocolate Dandies* in 1924 by the African–American choreographer Charlie Davis, and she attests that 'teams of black acrobatic tap dancers were a new trend on the Broadway stage in 1930' (p. 336). It wasn't until later that Irish dance was used to distinguish the Irish from the Africans and to represent their ethnicity as superior to other ethnicities, particularly African–American. This superiority is evident, she believes, in the *Riverdance* show *Live from New York City*. In her estimation the show was deeply influenced by African–American culture including Michael Jackson's *Moonwalk* dance, which concluded his virtuoso performance in the show. Yet Flatley continued to deny any African–American influences in his subsequent show, *Lord of the Dance*, and billed it as uniquely Irish (p. 337). He went one step further here. If, Carby (p. 337) argues, *Riverdance* can be criticised for its performance of 'discrete ethnicities, the cultural aesthetics of multiculturalism', then *Lord of the Dance* can be regarded as producing a 'cultural aesthetics of fascism' in which he proclaims the superiority of white over Black America. The narrative in this case revolves around the classic polarity between good/white and bad/black characters, the goodies being represented in the form of blonde colleens.

Carby sees *Riverdance* as reflecting a sense of Irishness ushered in by the Celtic Tiger. It is the result of the contradictions in Irish culture between the images of a historically oppressed nation on the one hand and a nation which had become the success story of the new Europe on the other. She claims that 'the fiction of *Riverdance* assertively presents a newly imagined Irish nationalism as evidence of its integration into the European Union and the new world order' and that the 'narrative purges the material conditions from which the cultural forms actually emerged, creating a new, improved, authentic and purified history' (p. 329). In creating this new identity in opposition to other identities, *Lord of the Dance* is both racialised and patriarchal:

> in all aspects of its staging, choreography, movement and sculpting of bodies, [the show] explicitly reproduces a form of mythology which reduces all social relations to a black and white dichotomy, a dichotomy which is, at one and the same time, a racialised and patriarchal narration of the traffic in women. (p. 343)

While the accounts above are all strongly critical of *Riverdance*'s immersion in a neoliberal, globalised culture, others are more positive and/or celebratory of Irishness. Fintan O'Toole (1997), journalist and cultural commentator, adopts a more liberal postmodernist approach to *Riverdance*, seeing it as an expression of a shift in Irish society from a puritanical and repressed culture to a creative and relatively liberating one in which Irish dance becomes sexy, exciting and exuberant. In his opinion, *Riverdance* is the confident artistic expression of the burgeoning economy – of a display of creativity and entrepreneurship in the arts – where traditional art forms are broken apart and reconstructed in an imaginative and innovative way. It is an example of Irish cultural expression overcoming a sense of post-colonial inferiority and confidently taking its place on the international stage.

Catherine Foley (2001, p. 39), coming from the perspective of a dancer, dance teacher and scholar, sees the globalisation of *Riverdance* as having a positive effect by 'positioning Ireland globally and culturally, representing a contemporary Irish identity to both the Irish themselves and to the world'. According to Foley (p. 41), the hybridity and inclusiveness of *Riverdance* have enabled the margins of Irish dance to come to the fore and she claims that 'the commodification of Irish step dance practice, particularly during the past five years, has acted as a major catalyst for the emergence of marginal dance practices and has reenergised the Irish step dance tradition' (p. 34). She gives the example of sean-nós dancing, which had been relegated to the margins of national culture pre-*Riverdance* but which had been revitalised by the show's success.[7]

The accounts considered above are diverse, both in terms of the aspects of globalisation they address and of their general conclusions, and ranging in tone from the sceptical and critical to the laudatory and celebratory. They are also partial, in that they don't take account of the meanings of *Riverdance* for audiences or the dancers themselves. While there has been some research on the experience of the dancers in *Riverdance* (e.g. see Wulff, 2005; Maguire, 2008), it has been a relatively neglected area of research.[8]

Globalisation and Cultural Identity: The Dancer and the Dance

With the purpose of engaging with dancers' experiential accounts and personal meanings of dance in the post-*Riverdance* era, I now draw on conversations I had with dancers in a *Riverdance*-style show. As already indicated, *Riverdance*'s success prompted the inclusion of either a single dancer or, most frequently, several dancers into their entertainment programmes. Although this type of cabaret/variety show had been in existence for many years in venues such as Dublin's Burlington Hotel, they increased dramatically post-*Riverdance*, when dancers became headline acts in the shows. The discussion that follows is based on conversations with seven female dancers and one male, between 16 and 23 years of age, in Mullen's pub in the Temple Bar area of Dublin in the summer of 2000. The objective of the discussions was to explore how they constructed meanings around their performance and, by inference, the kinds of cultural identifications that participation in the shows offered them. This piece of research is very limited in scope and cannot be taken as representative of show dancers in general – a task that would require more extensive and detailed research – but it is hoped that it can be instructive in some respects and raise relevant questions with regard to dance and identity in the global context.

The dancers believed that the influence of *Riverdance* was overall a positive one. Conversations revealed that the success of *Riverdance* internationally made step dance much more acceptable to their school classmates and friends, so that they no longer concealed the fact that they did Irish dancing. Irish step dance was now 'cool'. Martin, the sole male dancer in the show, commented on the fact that he used to get embarrassed at school but that now more people know about Irish dancing because they had probably seen *Riverdance* or other similar dance shows. Ciara commented that 'before, it was older people only who enjoyed Irish dancing; now everyone loves it and thinks you are great'. She too had previously concealed her dance activities from her schoolmates but reported that in her music class she would beat out the steps for classmates so that they could learn to differentiate between tunes such as the reel or the jig. They also reported that people they knew who had given up dancing were now resuming dance practice. This was also the case for a couple of the dancers themselves who had returned to dancing following *Riverdance*. Some of their friends and acquaintances regretted that they had not continued dancing because they wanted to join shows and it was easier to get into the shows if you were attached to a school of dancing. Dancers also wanted to get placed in competitions in order to progress to shows.

The dancers expressed a preference for performing in the shows over the competitions. From early childhood they had taken classes and competed with one of the two main step-dance organisations, the Coimisiún or the Comhdháil. Though the Comhdháil is seen to be somewhat more traditional than the Coimisiún, the diciplinary regime and competitive rivalry are legendary in both. Because competition dancing had been a vital element in their dancing 'careers' to date, they associated the solo dancing and the short three-minute performances of competition with high levels of stress. They enjoyed the performances for tourists and felt more relaxed because they thought that if they made a mistake in the footwork nobody would notice. Cathy commented: 'At feises you are being judged, people waiting for you to make a mistake.' Or Jenny: 'It has helped so much in confidence . . . it's completely different from feiseanna, where you are judged . . . here you are being complimented'. And Nuala adds: 'There is a different adrenalin rush here . . . [in feiseanna] the need to beat other people, here the adrenalin comes when the crowd get together.' They enjoyed the relaxed atmosphere and relative freedom associated with the show's performance contexts. However, there was an acknowledgement that the feiseanna can be enjoyable as well: 'You get to know lots of people and your friends are there cheering you on and then you cheer for them' (Martin). Dancing at the local/pub level generated a certain amount of camaraderie and cooperation and they enjoyed working with the other dancers and learning from each other. However, the competitive element continues to operate in terms of attempting to get into shows, whether for tourists, or top-level ones like *Riverdance*. This mix of cooperation and competition has been termed 'cooptition' by Jahner (2005) and is a central element in TV talent shows, another situation in which predominantly young people are engaged in artistic expression.

Audience response was a major element in their enjoyment of the shows and in their sense of themselves as dancers. Audiences were generally very appreciative of their performances and admired their dancing skills, which, in turn, generated a sense of self-confidence.[9] They were proud of their dancing skills, which, they were eager to point out, took years to learn. Martin said he felt 'proud because all those people are watching you and it makes you feel special . . . if the crowd has energy, it gives you more energy and the show is more enjoyable'. Another dancer remarked that the American audiences are looking for their roots and are eager to ask questions but that the appreciation is not confined to Americans; there are also Japanese tourists who have seen *Riverdance* and were so impressed that they wanted to see more. 'When you get a good crowd you dance well, you go home feeling good.' This kind of dynamic interaction between dancers and audience encourages them to perform well. Aoife commented: 'When the crowd are really into it, you get a great buzz. It is like that most of the time.' Caoimhe, too, thought that 'The audience entice you to dance well, especially when there are children in the audience, at weekends for instance. Or, if the crowd changes, you will want to dance well for the next crowd who haven't seen it before.'

The show's choreography was also strongly influenced by *Riverdance*. The majority of the audience, as tourists, would have gleaned their knowledge of Irish dance from *Riverdance* and this would have influenced their expectations of the shows. The dancers in Mullen's had a repertoire of about fifteen sets which included reels, jigs and hornpipes. However, they tended to favour hard-shoe dancing and faster rhythms because this was what they felt the audience preferred. Nuala commented: 'The crowd likes a quick beat and [we] enjoy doing it because the crowd likes it.' The show always began with a reel, because it was nice and lively and would engage the audience. Martin thought that 'the reels are generally the best because they are fast and noisy [they dance treble reels] . . . it is easier for the audience to get involved in reels. The hornpipe is slower and there is more emphasis on footwork and steps . . . more skill involved.' They would never start with a hornpipe, for instance, because it was too slow and the audience might not appreciate the intricacies of the footwork. They also included the 'stamping back' (a call and response sequence between the percussion musical instruments and rhythmic dancing without the musical accompaniment), which was a trade mark of *Riverdance* and which audiences really enjoyed. Some figures of a set dance were also included mainly because of the swing – 'not a proper set' – and adapted to suit the performance situation.

Other aspects of presentation were also influenced by *Riverdance*. The female dancers wore short black dresses and black tights, accentuating bodily contours. The sole male dancer wore plain black trousers and a black shirt. I have suggested elsewhere in relation to *Riverdance* (O'Connor, 1998, p. 57) that both male and female bodies were sexualised by the combination of soft materials, simple and figure-hugging costume design, and the dramatic effect of the colour black. The Mullen's dancers did not have the glitzy costumes of the lead dancers in *Riverdance,* but their style was a more muted version of the chorus line costumes in style and colour.

The subject of 'the smile' arose in conversation with respect to how dancers present themselves and they highlighted differences between the stage presentation of self that the national and the global systems generate. Jean, a Canadian dancer, reported that she was accustomed to smiling when she danced at feiseanna in Canada, but, since she learned that Irish dancers don't smile, she had stopped. She went on to tell the story of a feis adjudicator who deducted marks for smiling because it was seen as distracting. However, post-*Riverdance*, she mused, it is de rigueur to smile. I then asked other dancers about 'the smile'. Aoife does not tend to smile, as she learned not to do so in the feiseanna: 'In the feises you would be so scared you wouldn't smile because you are concentrating on getting everything perfect'. Another dancer, Caoimhe, was trained not to smile but, when she worked in the show in the Burlington Hotel, they were required to smile: 'Here [in Mullen's] it is more natural.' The show's organiser/manager did encourage dancers to move, smile, and be alert to the audience's reaction. Dancers were allowed a sense of agency and fun in what they were doing, while they were simultaneously encouraged to acknowledge that performances were audience-oriented.

Riverdance was seen to have had a positive influence on step dance because it had 'brought Irish dance into the public eye' and had created a demand for similar kinds of shows. They mentioned the increase in the number of shows, the opportunity to join a show, to travel internationally and, possibly, to provide a career. They saw as an added bonus the fact that they got paid for something which they regarded as fun. Prior to this, if one wanted to have a career in Irish dance, the only option was teaching, whereas now one could 'do a show'. Caoimhe regarded her situation as a reversal of the traditional order, where, instead of paying to go to dance classes, she got paid for dancing; for her it is a part-time job. She commented that while other friends and schoolmates had weekend and summer jobs too, they were not nearly as much fun. She had plans to go to Paris to study for a year and she intended to get a part-time job dancing in one of the Irish pubs in the city.[10]

While dancers were aware of the opportunities arising from the success of *Riverdance*, they were also critical of some of the more professional shows. Some referred to the more relaxed atmosphere of the pub shows and the more extreme regimen in the bigger shows. Stories circulated about long days of rehearsals with very little rest, dehydration and blisters, broken toes and limbs and situations where dancers were treated like 'a herd of cattle'. Triona spoke of her own experience of participating in workshops for one of the big shows, of how 'there were pools of water around the walls from the condensation, standing in line with numbers, so degrading'. Stories also circulated about girls who got kicked out for doing cocaine, and of the increasing emphasis on thinness and the increase in anorexia and bulimia among dancers. It was also thought that 'they treat you like machines, robots' in some shows, the last comment echoing the earlier critiques of 'mass spectacle' and demonstrating their awareness of the increasing commodification of dancers' bodies in these shows.[11]

Did performing Irish dance imbue dancers with a sense of Irishness? For the majority the sense of identity mobilised by their dancing seemed to be only incidentally related to a sense of Irishness. The exception was a Canadian dancer of Irish background who claimed that she had a sense of pride in her Irish identity. However, Ciara, one of the Irish-born dancers, reported that she didn't feel a sense of Irishness; that you don't have to be Irish to do Irish dancing and that a lot of English, American and Canadian girls do it. She reported that the two Canadian dancers in the Mullen's show always try to sound Irish when talking to tourists, because they [tourists] expect you to be an Irish 'colleen' type. Another dancer, Celine, said that she was so accustomed to doing Irish dancing that she just regarded it as a hobby. However, she did say (in response to a question) that she was proud to be Irish when she travelled to the USA on a five-week tour because the people they met were friendly, enthusiastic and very favourably disposed towards the Irish. Audiences approached the dancers to say how much they had enjoyed the show and the dancers got an opportunity to interact with people when selling brochures at the shows. Celine went on to say how they had green, white and gold costumes, which she initally thought were 'naff', but that she really liked them by the end of the tour. This anecdote illustrates very well how identification is not fixed but is rather mobilised in particular situations, in this case where Irishness was valorised by their hosts. It also highlights how identity formation is relational and continuously negotiated on the basis of other people's preconceived ideas of identity.

Dancers' motivation for working in Mullen's was an opportunity to combine (paid) work with fun, a sense of pride, of confidence in what they do, and the opportunity to travel abroad. The representation of work as fun is very much a part of the contemporary approach to work. The shows produce young, confident, skilled and mobile individuals – the kind of labour required by the global economy. The impact of globalisation is also manifest in the structure and style of the shows, where the customer/audience is king and where their expectations, based on their familiarity with *Riverdance*, influences the dancers' performance: the preferred dance style, the dancer's demeanour (expressed for example in the encouragement of smiling), the dance costumes and the preference for hard-shoe dances with maximum speed and percussion.

In many ways then *Riverdance*-style shows are part of a global entertainment industry determined by the mobility of the global economy and by the circuit of production and consumption involved. They require the global flow (Appadurai, 1996) of dancers and tourists. The dancers are employed as part of this mobile and flexible labour force. They don't have job security and, like ageing celebrity footballers, their shelf-life is short. The cost of training this highly skilled labour has not been borne by the producers of the shows but rather by the dancer's family. The costs include time inputs, classes (though the cost of the latter are relatively low), travel to feiseanna, and dance costumes and accessories that are relatively expensive. The shows are gaining the benefit of trained dancers, whose training takes place over the span of approximately fifteen years with most of the dancers starting classes at three or four years of age. The Coimisiún and the Comhdháil have been the two institutions to carry the responsibility for ensuring that the regimens of the body that are required for Irish step dancing are reproduced. It is worth noting in this context that the shows (global system) are feeding off the labour of the competitive (national) system (see Foley, 2001). Similar arguments have been made about reality TV shows that are also part of the globalised system of popular entertainment and some critics regard them as an exemplary case of bodies being turned into fodder for mass consumption (for example, see Ouellette and Hay, 2008).

Global Irishness?

Through its reflection on some of the contemporary meanings associated with *Riverdance* this chapter has engaged with the expression of a global Irish identity towards the end of the twentieth century. In summary it appears that the meanings of *Riverdance* and particularly the nature of its 'Irishness', which it both constitutes and reflects, are multiple and diverse. This 'global Irishness' (Rains, 2007, p. 132) was interpreted in a variety of ways by both critics and dancers, with some points of intersection and some areas of disagreement. For some, the kinds of identities reflected in and constituted by the show were seen as an unwelcome consequence of global capitalism. In these analyses Irish culture and economy are seen to be more interlinked and bound up with global developments than ever before and this relationship has been seen as affecting expressions of Irishness through dance. To summarise, Kavanagh et al. see it as reinforcing the work forms of a neo-liberal economy. Sherlock, while acknowledging the positive reinforcement of Irish identity in relation to the Irish diaspora, highlights the negative effects of its embeddedness in a globalised capitalist production regime. Carby views it as a racist expression of white Irish ethnicity. Alternatively O'Toole views *Riverdance* as an expression of freedom and confidence in a country that was coming of age in both cultural and economic terms, while Foley emphasises its positive effects in terms of the rejuvenation of local and marginalised dance cultures in Ireland.

As for the meanings attributed to step dance by the dancers, their experiential accounts also appear to be double-edged. It is clear that performing in Mullen's pub gave them a welcome opportunity to do something that was fun in an uncritical environment – an opportunity they would not have had if *Riverdance* had not happened. Through their performance they experienced a sense of confidence, of freedom, of appreciation and of pride. However, a macro-analysis suggests that their flexibility, mobility and skill, as well as the transformation of work into fun, make them suitable for a work environment in which each of these elements just happens to be an ideal personal requirement for the labour market in a neo-liberal economy. There is no easy way to choose between the opposing interpretations and it is important to acknowledge that the meanings constructed around Irish identity through *Riverdance*, whether analytic or experiential, are contingent. Given this divergence, it is difficult to answer the question posed at the beginning of the chapter as to whether Irish identity as expressed through dance at the end of the twentieth century was qualitatively different from that at the beginning. There is no doubt that the performance context of theatrical step dance is subject to the constraints imposed by global capitalism in the form of cultural markets as outlined above. However, the other side of the interpretive coin reveals a pride, a confidence and a sense of cultural achievement, the rejuvenation of other marginalised dance forms, and the sense of freedom and joyful exuberance expressed by the dancers themselves. It is all of these identifications, positive and negative, macro and micro, that form part of the complex of meanings surrounding *Riverdance*. Global Irishness as expressed through dance has the potential to be mobilised for consumer capital through spectacle, sensation and technically brilliant performances for mass entertainment. It also has the potential to break through the constraints imposed by the commodity culture and to be as genuinely creative, innovative and exciting as the original performance of *Riverdance* in 1994.

CHAPTER EIGHT

On With the Dance

Concluding Thoughts

This book set out to examine some aspects of the role of dance in the Irish cultural sphere at various points in time over the course of the twentieth century. Focusing on dance discourses and on social and theatrical dance performance, it explored how Irish dancing bodies negotiated a range of cultural identities: national and global, gender and social class, as well as ethnic in a diasporic context. Dance, it was argued, as an embodied cultural practice and mode of communication both reflected and constituted the Irish social and cultural sphere in which it was practised. In addition to being mediated through the social, cultural and political institutions in Irish society, it was also a way of performing that culture. The main line of argument throughout the book was that through dance forms, discourses and practices cultural identities were continuously produced and challenged. What, finally, can be said about the mediation of these identities, and the continuities and changes in these forms of identification over the course of the century?

Because of the large scope of the phenomena addressed as well as the diversity of topics covered there is no grand narrative to relate. However, there are a number of themes that are worthy of note. Identification with some form of Irishness was a theme running through many of the chapters. In the early decades of the century we witnessed how the Gaelic League sought to promote a distinctive sense of national identity through dance. Drawing on what was considered authentic and distinctive in the folk-dancing tradition, the new dance canon set out to create a perfect match between the Irish body politic and the Irish dancing body. The League's ability to enthuse and mobilise supporters on the ground to dedicate themselves to learning and transmitting the new dances through classes, competitions and social dance events indicates a nationwide enthusiasm for their efforts. And their success in establishing a flourishing tradition of Irish céilí dance for at least the next fifty years is testimony to the widespread support for their efforts. Although the development of céilí created distinctions between Irish and non-Irish dance, and in so doing tended to marginalise other dance traditions such as sets, its overall impact appears to have been a powerful and positive one as energiser of the Irish nation.

The creation of Irish national identity though dance became a source of struggle and conflict soon after the foundation of the independent Irish state, when the dominant discourse on dance was marked by the erection of a boundary between Irish/traditional dance and foreign/modern dance. The cultural and political power brokers of the era, believing that the latter were a threat to the moral state of the nation, sought to ban them. In so doing they were attempting to impose their own normative version of Irish identity. However, this version was opposed by the dancing public who identified with British and American popular music. Many disputed the view that it was necessary to avoid foreign, modern, or jazz dancing and felt that one could have a strong sense of Irish identity without restricting oneself to céilí dancing. Here we see an example of the struggle over claims to Irish national identity between cultural, religious and political power-brokers and ordinary citizens.

The Gaelic League was much more successful in its approach to the promotion of Irish dance in the early part of the century than in its draconian campaign against the 'jazzers' of the 1920s and 1930s. While boundary creation operated in both instances in terms of defining the nation through the distinction between Irish and foreign dance, the former was a more positive, voluntaristic energiser of national sentiment, whereas the latter was more exclusive, moralistic and dogmatic and was responded to accordingly.

Dance also played an important role in expressing and reproducing ethnic identity in the multi-ethnic societies of the Irish diaspora. The popularity of Irish dance, whether in private houses, dancehalls, stage performances, dance classes, competitions or festivals in so many places where Irish emigrants settled, is testimony to its importance in emigrants' lives. The pleasures of hearing familiar music and dance and connecting with people from home in the Boston dancehall of the 1940s and 1950s, as recounted by Gedutis; of the feiseanna as a family day out in the USA, as described by Cullinane; the sense of pride in their Irish background expressed by the dancers in Leonard's account of Coventry and Liverpool in the 1990s; all of these point to the dual role of dance in building an Irish ethnic community in their place of residence as well as maintaining a strong symbolic connection with the Irish homeland. While first-generation migrants have a memory of home, for the majority of the Irish diaspora it is an imagined sense of Ireland that they have learned from previous generations, from media and from travel. However, not to overplay the role of dance in articulating a sense of Irishness among the diaspora, it must be remembered that there were many migrants who chose not to draw attention to their ethnicity, either because of prejudice and/or discrimination against the Irish or because the label did not carry sufficient cultural capital.

An implicit and explicit sense of Irishness was also present amongst the set-dance community discussed in Chapter Five. The explicit one was similar to the diasporic sense of home in that set dancing was also associated with an 'imagined community' of a mythic home, but in this instance it was imagined as those geographic locations in the south and west of the country where the set-dance tradition had been continuous throughout the century. Like the diasporic home, it set up a desire to return to the place of origin, the source of inspiration. This imagined home was in many respects an idealised rural community associated with continuity of tradition and intergenerational communication through dance. Even for those dancers who did not articulate a sense of a geographic or spiritual home, dancing provided them with a means of building community through participation in the dance. This sense of community was experienced as friendly and welcoming, communicative, egalitarian and co-operative. The cultural values that were invoked through the dance were seen as an alternative to those invoked in other dance contexts and in the wider social sphere. This sense of Irishness was mobilised as a resistance to the changing patterns of interaction and values of Irish society – the relative absence of physical contact, the increase in virtual communication, hierarchical social structures, the growing anonymity and individualism of contemporary urban living; in effect those ways of life germane to contemporary capitalist relations.

Returning once again to the two dance events at each end of the century, the first céilí in Bloomsbury Hall in 1897 and the first performance of *Riverdance* at the Point Depot in 1994, the question arises as to the similarities and differences between the Irishness represented and performed in each. It is clear that Irish step dance played a pivotal role as a distinctive expression of Irish culture in both. However, the céilí signalled the start of a dance development for predominantly national performance/consumption, whereas *Riverdance* was developed with a predominantly international audience in mind. The incorporation of Irish step dance into the global cultural industries leads to some extent to the commodification of dance in line with international audience tastes. Because of its placement in the global circuit of cultural production, its attractiveness may be short-lived and is likely to be superseded by another fashion or ethnic branding. It is uncertain whether the meanings and pleasures of performance for the dancers themselves invoked a strong sense of national pride. True, there was a real sense of pride and confidence in performance but this seemed to be derived more from their dancing skills and their awareness of possessing a valuable but relatively scarce form of cultural capital that could also be turned into economic capital. It may be that Irishness was for them a more strategic and reflexive identity and more dependent upon the contingencies of the global culture industries. Following de Nora, dance was used for 'being' and 'doing' but perhaps not for 'feeling' Irish.

Critical interpretations of *Riverdance* were diverse and contradictory in terms of how Irishness was represented by the show. For some it was a positive marker of Irishness, strongly symbolic of an economically successful and creative nation, or as a means of encouraging the revival of hitherto marginalised dance forms. For others it represented a negative symbol of Irishness expressing either racism towards other cultures or the relations of capitalist cultural production during the Celtic Tiger era.

In the light of the evidence above regarding the commodification of step dance, it is tempting to claim that the sense of national identity as articulated through dance is lessening and in the long term will go into decline. However, this is premature and there are two points worth making in this regard. One is that the small number of dancers to whom I spoke may be atypical. And it is worth bearing in mind that dance could invoke diverse forms and strengths of identification with Irishness in the same decade. Riverdancers and set dancers, for instance, were both flourishing in the mid-1990s and it could be claimed that the global Irishness represented in the former was precisely what was being resisted in the latter. Age may also have been a factor in the relative strength of identification with Irishness in each case. The set dancers were older than the Mullens dancers and more engaged in civic culture and the public sphere, possibly leading to a greater sense of national identification. If that were so, the relative weakness of the latter's identification with Irishness could be partially attributed to their youth. It is also important to acknowledge that while some theatrical shows are embedded within the global culture industries, most of Irish step-dance practice continues to operate and flourish outside of this system. Contrary views and speculation make it impossible to form an easy overview of the play of Irish identities through dance over the course of the century. However, it is clear that the label 'Irish' was neither an essential or immutable category but was invoked in varying ways in relation to various social processes including those of national development, emigration and globalisation.

Dance was also found to be a barometer of changing social-class relations and identities in a number of dance contexts. Irish dance in the Gaelic Revival was coming out from the shadow of British colonialism. While leaders of the Gaelic League were attempting to develop a distinctive sense of Irishness through dance, they also sought the respectability that the colonial stereotype of the Irish as rowdy and uncivilised denied. Readers are reminded here of the ways in which the urban middle-class backgrounds of the leaders of the Gaelic League influenced their choice of dances for the new Irish dance canon and, in the process, how they rejected urban working-class culture as well as the more raucous, wild or bawdy aspects of the rural folk-dance culture in their selection.

Dance was also used to augment cultural capital and social status among Irish emigrants. In the diasporic situation social class and ethnicity were frequently interlinked. Irish emigrants to the USA sought to attain respectability by taming Irish music and dance in at least two ways. They did so by gradually distancing themselves from the music and dance of other ethnic groups, particularly African–Americans. They also sought to appeal to the middle classes. One instance of the shift towards the middle classes was the introduction of a seated audience for Irish dance music, and in so doing constraining movement and producing 'docile' bodies. This was as much the case for dance in Britain as in the USA, where taking Irish dance classes was a mark of respectability and was used as a strategy to counteract the association of the Irish with a less than respectable and predominantly male pub culture.

While identification with Irish music and dance for some was a means of achieving respectability by engaging in moderate and 'civilised' leisure, for others improvement in social status was achieved by maintaining their distance from Irish dance, as witnessed in Gedutis's account of the Irish dancehalls of Boston. Despite this, the overall evidence points to dance as aspirational in terms of social status and as a strategy for achieving integration into the host culture.

Dance was also a site of changing social class (as well as gender relations) for the ballroom dancers of the 1940s and 1950s. One of the primary ways of representing one's social-class identification, whether real or aspirational, was through consumption. Dance events promoted a consumption ethos on the part of female dancers in particular and provided them with an opportunity to display their consumption choices. The distinction created between local, rural and spartan dance venues and their relatively more luxurious, and sometimes though not always urban counterparts, signalled social-class distinction. Entrance fees were higher, appropriate dress and transport were generally more expensive, as was the production of the dance venue itself as an attractive, modern and comfortable space. A dancer's choice of venue was part of a more general identification with the urban as a centre of consumption and a corresponding rejection of the rural and the local as lacking the consumption choices they wished to make and the opportunity to achieve the social status to which they aspired.

If dance was a mark of distinction in social-class terms for the ballroom dancers, the converse was the case for the set dancers. In fact, it could be argued that the social–class–urban–consumption nexus apparent in the ballroom situation was reversed in the set-dance context. Here social class was seen to be irrelevant and one of its main pleasures was the breaking down of social distinctions and the creation of an egalitarian community of dancers. Set dancers also expressed an anti-consumption ethos to the extent that the dance was seen to be characterised by simplicity and naturalness, associated with folk dancing generally. There was also a gravitational pull towards local and rural dance in the case of some of the set dancers, unlike the ballroom dancers, who wished to distance themselves from the rural as socially and culturally backward.

Gender identities were strongly articulated through dance over the course of the century and gender relations were embedded in various ways in dance discourse and performance. This was apparent in the separate dance regimes for men and women in the early years of the century, in dominant discourses on modern dance and in the changing gender roles for Irish step-dance teaching and performance in the 1920s and 1930s, as well as in the gendered dance pleasures of both ballroom and set dance. From the early dance manuals we saw how dance regimes were gendered, with rules for the appropriate movement of male and female dancing bodies, of a dancing style encouraging lightness and grace for women and strength and complexity for men. The transition in step-dance performance from a gender-mixed activity to a predominantly female one was complete by the 1930s. The young female dancing body became the object of the public gaze and valorised as symbolic of Irish national identity. Despite the increased popularity of step dance for boys post-*Riverdance*, the gendering of Irish step dance continues into the present, where the participation rate of girls and young women far outnumbers that of boys and young men. From the 1930s on, step-dance teaching was also to become a predominantly female activity, a transition that can be linked to the changing role of women in the public sphere. Arguably, this would have negatively affected the number of boys taking up dance. Furthermore, ambivalence existed around male dancing bodies, as there was a belief, still current, that there was greater scope for the expression of masculinity on the sports field than on the dance floor. The gradual shift from male to female in step dance was double-edged in terms of gender norms. It manifested the dominant ideology about women's primary role, in so far as teaching was seen as an extension of women's 'natural' maternal role of caring for children. At the same time it enabled female teachers to actively participate in the public sphere and to have a measure of economic independence. Likewise for the dance performers, who were at one and the same time objectified in the public (male?) gaze while actively participating in a pleasurable and powerful activity.

While it was acceptable for the 'traditional' Irish dancing woman to be in the public gaze, this was not the case for the 'modern' dancing woman. This character who represented an alternative role for women, who dressed in contemporary fashion, wore make-up and danced to modern/jazz music in the public dancehalls was a particular target of patriarchal ire and was persistently criticised by political, cultural and church leaders throughout the 1920s and 1930s. The 'threatening mobilities' of the modern dancing woman were derived from the dominant view of women's dual sexual nature as virgin/whore, leading them to be regarded as simultaneously vulnerable and dangerous. This created ambivalence around their occupying public space and especially the dancehall space where they were in close physical proximity to men. The moral panic that developed at this time around women and dance was based on public anxieties about women's sexuality, reproduction and 'illegitimacy'.

Gender identities also formed around specific dancing forms and pleasures. The form of ballroom dance itself reflected the gradual transition from an extended family structure symbolised by group dance to a nuclear one symbolised by closed-couple dancing with the male lead representing his position as head of the family. Women negotiated new forms of gendered identities through the dancehall space. In some ways it was a bounded and special space, separated out from the quotidian, and produced as glamorous and romantic. But it was also a space in which everyday dramas could be acted out, in this case the drama of romance. Consumption (discussed in terms of social class identifications above) played a part in these staged romantic dramas. The purchase of clothes and accessories was seen as mandatory and confirmed the general importance of self-presentation for women as object of the male and female gaze. Women performed their feminine identity through fashion which, following the Second World War, was intended to emphasise the hyper-feminine in a bid to re-establish the pre-war status quo with regard to gender roles. Dances also brought gender relations into play. Preparation for dances was frequently an occasion of all-female camaraderie that was interrupted later on by competition for men's attention and rivalry for dance partners. However, gendered identities were not associated exclusively with dance pleasures and women were aware of the limits of the romantic utopia of the dancehall and of the realities of gender inequities.

Gendered pleasures of dance were also apparent in set dancing and, although the pleasures of set dance were for the most part common to men and women, there were some that were specific to each. Women reported that that they felt safer in the set-dance environment than in other dance situations they had experienced. This was not an issue for men. Women also referred to the fact that they could attend without a partner, and were free to come and go as they wished. Their greater sense of autonomy than the ballroom dancers of the earlier decades is a reflection of the relatively greater equality for women in Irish society in the 1990s. However, it is worth noting that the sense of freedom experienced in set dance did not apply to all dance situations as indicated in their critique of disco, where gender relations were seen to be more problematic.

Discussion and analysis of the interwoven themes of identities in the book has been informed by the three overarching and interrelated concepts of power, meaning and pleasure. Regulatory institutional power was clearly apparent in the bid by voluntary institutions – primarily the Gaelic League; religious institutions in particular the Catholic Church; and political institutions of the state – to control dance and to decide what dance forms, behaviour and venues were to be encouraged or forbidden. However, as we saw, this power play was met with resistance on the part of the dancing public, indicating that power is constantly being struggled over and that the cultural politics of dance is relational. While the institutional power of cultural institutions was more apparent in the early twentieth century, more recently, following the incorporation of dance into a global cultural economy, economic institutions have come to exercise more regulatory power over dance, as witnessed in the discussion of *Riverdance*.

Dance power was also frequently experienced as dancing pleasure. Some of these pleasures were common, such as the exuberance and joy of the dance movement itself. A sense of self-mastery, accomplishment and self-transcendence was also clearly conveyed in conversations with ballroom, set dancers and tourist-show dancers alike. However, there were also differences in dancing power/pleasure that were contingent on the performance context. The romantic pleasures of ballroom were associated with dancers' power to attract men and their popularity as a dance partner. Set dancers experienced the power and pleasure of producing a sense of community with others in the set. The sense of power of the show dancers was inextricably linked to their engagement with an audience appreciative of the high level of dancing skills. At a micro level the felt absence of power was expressed through anxieties and tensions around dance: the tension between the desire for romance and awareness of the realities of women's relative lack of power in ballroom dancing, or the anxieties expressed by male and female set dancers about their inability to control communication in the disco-dance situation.

Dance, like other bodily movements, carried meanings that were continuously constructed in Irish public culture in general as well as by dancers themselves. We have seen, for example, how the dancing Irish colleen accumulated meanings around her to become a symbol of the Irish nation in nationalist discourse at the turn of the twentieth century. We have also witnessed how modern/jazz dance carried dominant moral and medical meanings, of being both sinful and unhealthy in the Ireland of the 1920s and 1930s. Meanings may change over time, as we have observed in relation to the ways in which set dance accrued meanings around the context of its perform-ance in the city in the 1990s as opposed to the country in the 1930s. For dancers, meanings and pleasures were frequently interlinked. However, a disjuncture between meanings and pleasures was also evident and was expressed, for example, in the insider/outsider views of set dancers when the stereotype they had of dancers as middle-aged and lonely was offset by the sheer enjoyment of the dancing itself. The differences in the meanings of *Riverdance* both in the critical scholarly accounts and between those and the personal accounts of the dancers serve as a reminder that meanings, no more than power or pleasure, are not fixed but that the process of interpretation is a con-tinuous and contested one.

As with dance, the shape of this book was determined by the context of its production. I am conscious of the limited scale of my own empirical research compared with the large scope of the phe-nomena addressed and that some of the questions raised cannot be satisfactorily answered. Writing the book presented a number of methodological challenges too. These included the absence of basic records on social dancing and an imbalance between data sources. There is, for instance, a substantial body of writing on the institu-tional control of dance for the 1920s and 1930s. This wealth of documentation on the normative moral and legal issues surrounding dance is due principally to the fact that local and national newspapers reported and sometimes reproduced verbatim the pronouncements on dance by the Catholic Church, often in the form of Lenten Pastorals, as well as reports of the public discussion at local and national government level. The latter is also supplemented by publicly accessible archives on the Dáil debates on the Dance Hall's Act of

1935 as well as the legislation itself. The reliance on almost exclusively official documentary sources on dance regulation generates a normative discussion of dance. In contrast the relative dearth of information on the practices and experiences of dancers themselves leads to an imbalance between normative and experiential writing on dance for this particular era. I have tried to correct this imbalance where possible by including dancers' accounts of their experiences. Since the time of writing, it is encouraging to see the increase in resources for dance research in Ireland. The recent opening of a National Dance Archive at the Academy of World Music and Dance in the University of Limerick is heartening in this respect.

It is also the case that the analysis is based more on women's than on men's experience of dancing. I also experienced great difficulty in accessing the most basic statistical data on recreational dance such as the number of public dance venues in Ireland at any particular point in time. Thom's Directory does not include information on commercial premises, but even if it had it would not necessarily have solved the problem because of the multi-purpose nature of many dance venues. There was some data available on the amount of revenue generated through entertainment duty on dances ('dance tax') but this is also difficult to interpret because it was aggregated with other data. In this respect, too, the relative absence of dance statistics adds to the difficulty of building up basic information at a national level on recreational dance.

The book is clearly not, nor is intended to be, a comprehensive account of dance over the course of the twentieth century. Themes are selective and not systematically pursued through each chapter. It would have been useful, for example, to follow the theme of urban modernity introduced in Chapter Four into the showband era of the 1960s. It might have complemented Vincent Power's very engaging and informative book, *Send Them Home Sweatin'*, on the showbands themselves. However, this would have entailed more extensive empirical research than was feasible. Other dance forms and subcultures associated with particular decades also deserve attention: rock and roll in the late 1950s and early 1960s, break dancing in the 1980s, as well as the wide variety popular at the end of the century such as hip-hop, tango, salsa and capoiera. It is hoped that other scholars will be encouraged by these absences to develop a more extensive and robust body of dance knowledge.

Future dance research calls for a broad range of methodologies and research techniques: structural/formal analyses of dance, observation of dance events, interviews and conversations, as well as relevant quantitative data and analyses of texts and images. Theoretical interdisciplinarity, including areas of scholarship such as cultural history and geography, sociology and anthropology, dance and performance studies, would also be welcome. Approaches from other research areas such as media/communication studies might also be useful. This would ideally entail an integrated approach to production, text and consumption and, applied to dance, would include economies of dance production, performance/practice, representation of dance in written and visual texts such as film and television, as well as dance audiences. Currently the research emphasis is on performance and representation while the production and consumption aspects are relatively neglected.

Substantive and methodological weaknesses aside, it is hoped that this volume will help to bring what was a relatively 'unmarked' (Phelan, 1993) aspect of popular culture into the foreground and stimulate further reflection on the power, meanings and pleasures of dance in Irish culture.

Notes

1 THE IRISH DANCING

1 Celtic Tiger cubs is the expression commonly given to the children of those who benefited from the relatively short-lived 'boom' of the Irish economy in 1996–2007 approximately.

2 THE BODY POLITIC

1 This dual response is well captured in Memmi's book *The Colonizer and the Colonized* (1965), an analysis of colonialism in Tunisia. It generates a situation in which the colonised wish on the one hand to reject the colonial 'other' while simultaneously mimicking their behaviour.

2 It was not until the setting up of An Coimisiún that a compromise was agreed. An Coimisiún was charged with overseeing 'the evolution of the dance form by controlling its rate of change and its stability through a system of exclusive competitions coupled with a programme for official certification of dance teachers' (Meyer, 2001, p. 71).

3 It is interesting to note that Munster and especially Kerry was the base for developing canons in Irish language and literature around the same time (for example, see Nic Eoin, 2003).

4 Seoníní is the plural of the Irish word 'seonín' or 'seánín', translated into English as 'little John' or John Bull, the symbolic figure of Britishness. It is a term of derision for those who ape foreign manners and customs.

5 Connerton (1989) applies the distinction between natural and forced bodily ease to social class positions and is in this regard similar to Bourdieu's (1984) work on how social class position can be inferred through bodily orientations or 'habitus'.

6 Aeríocht is Irish for an open-air event and scoruigheacht for an indoor event. McMahon (2008, p. 165) informs us that at 'these spirited sessions, branch members [of the Gaelic League] or students from area schools typically performed short plays and musical numbers alongside local enthusiasts and nationally known Irish-Irelanders, who delivered addresses designed to stir up support for the movement'.

7 The park fêtes were celebrations rather than competitions. This was in contrast to both the competitive nature of Irish step dance and to the New York boys' leisure that featured competitive athletics as early as 1903 (see Tomko, 1996). The early presence of the competitive element in Irish step dance raises questions about its effect on young female dancers of the era and on the overall cultural climate of step dance.

8 Commonplace but telling examples are incorporated into the monopoly men had on playing traditional musical instruments, particularly the higher status, more technologically sophisticated and more expensive ones such as the fiddle and the uileann pipes. Women were confined (with notable exceptions such as the concertina) to the technologies of the body, expressed in singing and dancing (for further details, see Vallely, 2011).

3 THE DEVIL IN THE DANCEHALL

1 I have not yet established whether the infamous dances such as the Shimmie and the Charleston, both objects of concern in Britain at this time, were commonly danced in Ireland.

2 Pen name for D. Breathnach.

3 Much of the normative writing on social dance relates to this period. It is interesting to note that the wealth of information is due to the availability of official state records or the reproduction in national and provincial newspapers of the pronouncements of the Catholic hierarchy on dance. These documents illustrate the power of both institutions to influence the legal and moral discourses on dance at this time.

4 Fr Devane was a member of the Carrigan Committee and expressed alternative opinions to the other (five) members of the Roman Catholic clergy on the committee. One such opinion was about the 'dual standard of morality accepted in this country, as in perhaps no other, where the woman is always hounded down and the man dealt with leniently' (quoted in Smith, 2004, p. 221).

5 This trend was most explicitly expressed in the Constitution of 1937 in which women's primary role was constructed as mothers within the home which, *inter alia*, led to the implementation of the 'marriage bar', which denied married women access to public service jobs.

6 It is likely, given the double standards regarding sexuality, that women would have been more compliant than men. There was probably also a social class dimension in that respectability was highly valued amongst the middle classes. There may in addition have been a geographical dimension, as suggested in Kevin Whelan's (1988) claim that after the Famine piety was more common among the middle classes of Munster and Leinster than in Connacht, where there was widespread anti-clericism.

7 The duty on admissions to dances fluctuated over the forty-year period in which it was in operation. The highest amount of £129,257 was collected in 1959. There was also a steady increase from £15,700 in 1940 to £54,517 in 1946. The tax was revoked in 1946 and reintroduced in 1949, only to be

removed again in 1952 and reimposed in 1956. Exemptions on entertainment duty included those held in rural areas, those for charitable or educational purposes and those promoting the Irish language. It was finally abolished because it was felt that it discriminated against cinema and dances in cities and larger towns.

4 BALLROOMS OF ROMANCE

1 My own conversations with dancers indicate that they were allowed to go to 'céilís' (though 'céilithe' is the correct plural, I use the vernacular) when they were young. They were seen as more appropriate for younger dancers as they were more regulated and thus regarded as safer by their parents. Dancers moved on to modern dances as they got older and generally developed a preference for them.
2 Britain and the USA also witnessed a rapid increase in the number of dancehalls in the 1930s.
3 Entertainment tax returns give aggregate figures for a number of years but these are difficult to interpret.
4 While Illouz (1997) also includes the exchange of ritual words of love as an element within the staged drama of romance, the latter would have been substantially absent in the dance context under discussion.
5 Men's reluctance to ask women to dance seems to have continued on throughout the century. A male caller to the *Gay Byrne Show* (RTÉ, 9 February 1996) complained about one particular rural ballroom he knew where he said the men sat around all night instead of asking girls to dance.
6 For more information on the political context in which Jim Gralton's dance hall was forced to close, see Gibbons (1996).
7 Langhamer (2000), in her study of women's leisure in the interwar years in England, notes that consumption was an important aspect of dancehall culture.
8 While radio listening may in theory be regarded as a leisure practice, for many women in the home work and leisure practices were combined.
9 A typical example is the announcement of the opening of a ladies' hairdressing saloon and beauty parlour in Carrick-on-Shannon where the proprietor indicates that she is 'late of MR A. PALCIC'S [note the capitalisation], Grafton Street, Dublin' and where 'All Modern Machinery and Equipment, as used by the leading Dublin Hairdressers will be employed' . . . and where 'Patrons are assured of Personal Attention and Efficiency' (*Leitrim Observer*, 25 August 1934).
10 According to Ferriter (2005, p. 430), twenty-two million cinema tickets were purchased in Ireland in 1943.
11 The film *Ballroom of Romance*, directed by Pat O'Connor (1982) and based on the short story by William Trevor, portrays very vividly the differential gender involvement in the discourse of romance among the dancegoers in the ballroom.
12 Zygmunt Bauman (1990, p. 64) notes the importance of dress in terms of

identity formation, claiming that 'dress has acquired the role of one of the prime symbolic devices used by men and women to make a public statement about the reference group they have chosen as their pattern, and the capacity in which they wish to be perceived and approached'.

13 This feeling is not confined to the era under discussion. A feminist colleague of mine who went to ballroom classes in the 1990s told me that one of the pleasures of having a man lead was that it provided her with the opportunity for temporarily shedding the sense of responsibility associated with the management of her busy working day.

14 The same feeling of transcendence, though in a different performance context, is beautifully captured in Elizabeth Bowen's (1942, p. 93) account of learning to waltz as a child. After several weeks of clumsy perseverance, she recounts, she finally finds herself able to waltz: 'a spring released itself in my inside. My feet and body release themselves, without warning, from inside the noose of my consciousness. Like a butterfly free of the chrysalis, like a soul soaring out of the body, I burst from the file of duffers and went spinning smoothly, liquidly round the floor by myself. I waltzed. The piano dropped its disdainful note and quickened and melted in sympathy. I felt no floor under my feet: this was my dream of being able to fly. I could fly – I could waltz.'

5 RETURN OF THE REPRESSED?

1 It is frequently claimed that set dance reached the height of its popularity in the mid-1990s. However, it continues to be popular especially among older age groups.

2 A number of the people to whom I spoke about set dancing are no longer involved in the community, supporting the point that these new communities of interest are constantly changing.

3 The socio-demographic characteristics of the people to whom I spoke cannot be seen as statistically representative of the set-dance population. However, in terms of social class Hall (1994) also found that enthusiasm for set dancing in England was greatest among the lower-middle-class Irish and British–Irish during the 1980s.

4 These findings are similar to Finnegan's (1989) study of musicians in Milton Keynes, where they knew little about people's lives outside the community created by the musical performance.

5 The age inclusiveness of set dance is confirmed by O'Connor (1991, p. 90) with reference to the USA. In contrast to step dancing, it involved young and old and afforded a wide range of people the possibility of expressing themselves through traditional music in social situations.

6 The set-dance situation was not wholly positive for women. Some mentioned restraints on their behaviour, such as the difficulty of refusing a dance because of the likelihood of meeting the same person again.

7 Though impossible to verify from my own research, the aspect of 'getting it right' seemed to be more important to men than to women. Women also seemed less bothered than men about making mistakes (breaking the rules),

whereas some men expressed a desire to build up competence and confidence before dancing in public.

8 The dancers who talked most about the association of set dance with an idyllic rural community were women. However, I don't know if this is significant and, if so, how to interpret the gender difference.

9 This may have a special relevance for women. I have frequently heard women comment that they love dancing but don't have the opportunities to dance that they had in their youth. Set dancing provided this opportunity and may well be one of the reasons for its popularity amongst older women.

6 DANCING THE DIASPORA

1 Hendrikson (1984, p. 11) surmises that the reason may be that the Irish jigs were 'probably more joyous and carefree than the Scottish or English' with names such as *Smash the Window, Pretty Girl Milking her Cow, The Growling Old Woman, Barney, Leave the Girls Alone*!

2 Cullinane (1997) reports that, while most overseas Irish dancers and teachers are first- or second-generation Irish, many have no Irish connections. Often they are attracted to Irish dancing by the strong Irish influence in their neighbourhood or in the schools.

3 This might be illustrated by comparing the relative number of Irish music and dance entertainers on the American stage in the early years of the century with those in British stage shows of the same period. British music hall for example catered to working-class and lower middle-class cultural tastes and were very popular amongst those classes in Dublin (see Rockett, 1990). Middle to highbrow figures such as Oscar Wilde seem to have had more of an impact on British culture of this era.

7 THE *RIVERDANCE* EFFECT

1 There is a substantial body of literature on *Riverdance* from a variety of perspectives but it is beyond the scope of this chapter to address it.

2 The increased emphasis on dance as a commercial cultural product is the result of the close link between culture and economy as part of a more general process of de-differentiation of societal spheres.

3 See O'Connor (2012) for a discussion of the importance of bodily movement of participants in television talent shows.

4 Bordo's (1993) feminist analysis of the 'mass ornamental movement' argues against dominant interpretations that claim that dancers are totally divested of power. Alternatively she suggests that performances by women dancers simultaneously express ideals of enjoyable, healthy physical activity that are the antithesis of notions of female delicacy.

5 See Ó Cinnéide (2002) for an account of the economics of the production of *Riverdance*.

6 Similar arguments about global production standards are made in relation to other forms of popular global entertainment. With reference to television talent shows, for example, Coutas (2006) speaks of the production of 'global

glamour', which is largely determined by the technological facilities for creating high production values.

7 With reference to the local/global dynamic O'Connor (1991, p. 88) notes that, when the recordings of fiddlers Michael Coleman and James Morrison came back to Ireland from America, they had a profound impact on musical style and dance repertoire in Ireland. This led to the predominance of the reel over jigs and hornpipes. Dances such as slides, polkas, mazurkas, schottisches and highlands got little if any airing. The movement started by O'Neill with the publication of *Dance Music of Ireland* was consolidated by the emulation of Coleman and Morrison. These local/global interactions resulted in a downgrading of regional playing and the predominance of the Sligo style.

8 It may seem surprising that, despite the amount of critical attention *Riverdance* has received, there has not been a systematic study of the popular responses to it. The optimum moment for this kind of research would have coincided with the show's initial runs and it may now be a bit late to capture the freshness and excitement of its early days. Nonetheless, it would still be a valuable exercise to explore this important element of dance history.

9 Moya Kneafsey (2003) also found that musicians reported that tourists attending traditional Irish music sessions in pubs in County Mayo showed a greater appreciation of the musical performances than the locals.

10 Irish dancing in an Irish theme pub in Paris is a good example of the interlocking of various dimensions of Irish culture in the service of the global branding of Irishness.

11 It is only fair to point out that criticism of the professional shows is not universal. In another context a former dancer with *Riverdance* told me her experience of dancing with the company was totally positive. She recalled the whole experience with fondness and as one of the most enjoyable times in her life.

Bibliography

Please note, Mc is treated as Mac.

Abbott, Phillip, *Seeking Many Inventions*. Knoxville: University of Tennessee Press, 1987.

Abrahams, R.D., 'Phantoms of Romantic Nationalism in Folkloristics', *Journal of American Folklore*, vol. 106, 1993, pp. 3–37.

Adair, C., *Women and Dance: Sylphs and Sirens*. London: Macmillan, 1992.

Anderson, Benedict, *Imagined Communities*. London: Verso, 1983.

Anelius, Josephus, *National Action: A Plan for the National Recovery of Ireland* (2nd edition). Dublin: Gaelic Athletic Association, 1943.

Appadurai, Arjun, *Modernity at Large: Cultural Dimensions of Globalization*. Minneapolis: University of Minnesota Press, 1996.

Austin, Valerie A., 'The Ceili and the Public Dance Halls Act, 1935', *Eire–Ireland*, vol. 28 no. 3, pp. 7–16.

Back, Les, 'Nazism and the Call of the Jitterbug', in H. Thomas (ed.), *Dance in the City*. London: Macmillan, 1997.

Bakhtin, Mikhail, *Rabelais and his World*. Trans. Hélène Iswolsky. Bloomington: Indiana University Press, 1993.

Bauman, Zygmunt, *Thinking Sociologically*. Oxford: Blackwell, 1990.

___, 'From Pilgrim to Tourist: Or a Short History of Identity' in S. Hall and P. du Gay (eds.), *Questions of Cultural Identity*. London: Sage, 1996, pp. 18–36.

Berger, John, 'The Suit and the Photograph', in J. Berger, *About Looking*. New York: Pantheon Books, 1980.

Blacking, John, 'Towards an Anthropology of the Body', in J. Blacking (ed.), *The Anthropology of the Body*. New York: Academic Press, 1977.

Blanchard, Paul, *The Irish and Catholic Power*. Boston: The Beacon Press, 1953.

Boas, Franz, *The Function of Dance in Human Society*. New York: Dance Horizons, 1972.

161

Bordo, S., *Unbearable Weight: Feminism, Western Culture and the Body.* Berkeley: University of California Press, 1993.

Bottomley, Gillian, *From Another Place: Migration and the Politics of Culture.* Cambridge: Cambridge University Press, 1992.

Bourdieu, Pierre, *Distinction: A Social Critique of the Judgement of Taste.* London: Routledge, 1984.

___, *The Logic of Practice.* California: Stanford University Press, 1990.

Bowen Elizabeth, 'Dancing in Daylight', *The Bell*, vol. v, no. 2, 1942, pp. 90–8.

Brah, A., *Cartographies of Diaspora: Contesting Identities.* London: Routledge, 1996.

Breathnach, Brendán, *Folk Music and Dances of Ireland.* Cork: Mercier, 1977.

___, *Dancing in Ireland.* Milltown Malbay, Co. Clare: Dal gCais Publications, 1983.

Brennan, Helen, 'Reinventing Tradition: The Boundaries of Irish Dance', *History Ireland,* Summer, 1994, pp. 22–5.

___, *The Story of Irish Dance.* Dingle: Brandon, 1999.

Brown, Terence, *Ireland: A Social and Cultural History 1922–79.* London: Fontana, 1981.

Buckland, T.J., 'Dance, Authenticity and Cultural Memory: The Politics of Embodiment', *Yearbook for Traditional Music,* vol. 33, 2001, pp. 1–16.

Burt, R., *Alien Bodies: Representations of Modernity, 'Race', and Nation in Early Modern Dance.* London: Routledge, 1998.

Butler, Judith, *Bodies that Matter: On the Discursive Limits of 'Sex'.* London: Routledge, 1993.

Byrne, Helen, 'Going to the Pictures' in M.J. Kelly and B. O'Connor (eds.) *Media Audiences in Ireland: Power and Cultural Identity.* University College Dublin Press, 1997.

Carby, H.V., 'What Is This "Black" in Irish Popular Culture?', *Cultural Studies,* vol. 4, no. 3, 2001, pp. 325–49.

Casey, M.R., 'Before Riverdance: A Brief History of Irish Step Dancing in America', in J.J. Lee and M.R. Casey (eds.), *Making the Irish American: History and Heritage of the Irish in the United States.* New York: New York University Press. 2006, pp. 417–25.

Casey, Natasha, 'Riverdance: The Importance of Being Irish American', *New Hibernia Review/Iris Eireannach Nua,* vol. 6, no. 4, 2002, pp. 9–25.

Cinnéide, B.O., *Riverdance: The Phenomenon.* Dublin: Blackhall, 2002.

Cohen, Stanley, *Folk Devils and Moral Panics: Creation of Mods and Rockers* (3rd edition). London: Routledge, 2002.

Connerton, P. *How Societies Remember.* Cambridge University Press, 1989.

Coombes, Annie E., *Reinventing Africa: Museums, Material Culture and*

Popular Imagination in Victorian and Edwardian England. New Haven: Yale University Press, 1994.

Corcoran, Mary P., Jane Grey and Michel Peillon, *Suburban Affiliations: Social Relations in the Greater Dublin Area*. Dublin: University College Dublin Press, 2010.

Coulter, Colin, and Steve Coleman, *The End of Irish History? Critical Reflections on the Celtic Tiger*. Manchester: Manchester University Press, 2003.

Coutas, Penelope, 'Fame, Fortune, *Fantasi*: Indonesian Idol and the New Celebrity', *Asian Journal of Communication*, vol. 16, no. 4, 2006, pp. 371–92.

Cowan, Jane, *Dance and the Body Politic in Northern Greece*. Princeton: Princeton University Press, 1990.

Cresswell, Timothy, '"You Cannot Shake that Shimmie Here". Producing Mobility on the Dance Floor', *Cultural Geographies*, vol. 13, 2006, pp. 55–77.

Cronin, Michael, and Barbara O'Connor, 'From Gombeen to Gubeen: Tourism, Identity and Class in Ireland, 1949–1999', in R. Ryan (ed.), *Writing in the Irish Republic: Literature, Culture, Politics 1949–1999*. Houndmills: Macmillan, 2000, pp. 165–84.

Cronin, Mike, 'Sport and a Sense of Irishness', *Irish Studies Review*, vol. 3, no. 9, 1994/5, pp. 13–17.

Crouch, David, 'The Power of the Tourist Encounter', in A. Church and T. Coles (eds.), *Tourism, Power and Space*. London: Routledge, 2007, pp. 45–62.

Csikszentmihalyi, Mihalyi, *Flow: The Psychology of Optimal Experience*. New York: Harper Collins, 1991.

Culler, Jonathan, 'Semiotics of Tourism', *American Journal of Semiotics*, vol. 1, nos. 1–2, 1981, pp. 127–40.

Cullinane, John, 'Irish Dancers World-Wide: Irish Migrants and the Shaping of Traditional Irish Dance', in P. O'Sullivan (ed.), *The Creative Migrant: Vol. 3*. The Irish World-Wide: History, Heritage, Identity Series. Leicester: Leicester University Press, 1997.

Curtis, Liz, *Nothing But the Same Old Story: The Roots of Anti-Irish Racism*. London: Information on Ireland, 1984.

de Certeau, Michel, *The Practice of Everyday Life*. Berkeley: University of California Press, 1984.

de Lauretis, Teresa, 'Introduction: Feminist Studies/Critical Studies', in T. de Lauretis (ed.), *Feminist Studies/Critical Studies*. London: Macmillan, 1986, pp. 1–19.

de Nora, Tia, *Music in Everyday Life*. Cambridge: Cambridge University Press. 2000.

Desmond, Jane C., 'Embodying Difference: Issues in Dance and Cultural

Studies', in A. Carter (ed.), *The Routledge Dance Studies Reader*. Oxford: Routledge, 1998, pp. 154–62.

Devane, R.S., 'The Dance-Hall', *Irish Ecclesiatical Record*, February, 1931, pp. 170–94.

Dickens, Charles, *American Notes*. London: Chaucer Press, 1842.

Douglas, Mary, *Natural Symbols: Explorations in Cosmology*. London: Cresset Press, 1976.

Durkheim, Émile, *The Elementary Forms of Religious Life*. Trans. A.W. Swain. London: Allen & Unwin, 1915.

Dyer, Richard, *Only Entertainment*. London: Routledge, 1992.

Edensor, Tim, *National Identity, Popular Culture and Everyday Life*. Oxford: Berg, 2002.

Elias, Norbert, *The Civilising Process: State Formation and Civilization*. Oxford: Basil Blackwell, [1939] 1978.

Enloe, Cynthia, *Bananas, Beaches and Bases: Making Feminist Sense of International Politics*. London: Pandora, 1989.

Feintuch, B., 'Longing for Community', *Western Folklore*, vol. 60, nos. 2/3, 2001, pp. 149–61.

Ferriter, Diarmaid, *The Transformation of Ireland, 1900–2000*. London: Profile Books, 2005.

Finnegan, Ruth, *The Hidden Musicians*. Cambridge: Cambridge University Press, 1989.

Foley, Catherine, 'Perceptions of Irish Step Dance: National, Global, and Local', *Dance Research Journal*, vol. 33, no. 1, 2001, pp. 34–45.

Foucault, Michel, *The History of Sexuality, Vol. 1: An Introduction*. Harmondsworth: Penguin, 1981.

___, *Discipline and Punish: The Birth of the Prison*. Trans. Alan Sheridan. New York: Vintage, 1979.

Francmanis, J. 'National Music to National Redeemer: The Consolidation of a "Folk-Song" Construct in Edwardian England', *Popular Music*, vol. 21, no. 1, 2002, pp. 1–25.

Frank, W., 'For a Sociology of the Body: An Analytic Review', in M. Featherstone et al. (eds.), *Social Processes and Cultural Theory*. London: Sage, 1991, pp. 36–103.

Franko, M., *Dancing Modernism/Performing Politics*. Bloomington: Indiana University Press, 1995.

Friel, Mary, *Dancing as a Social Pastime in the South-East of Ireland, 1800–1897*. Dublin: Four Courts Press, 2004.

Garvin, Tom, *Nationalist Revolutionaries in Ireland, 1858–1928*. Oxford: Clarendon Press, 1987.

Gedutis, Susan, *See You at the Hall: Boston's Golden Era of Irish Music and Dance*. Boston: Northeastern University Press, 2004.

Gellner, Ernest, *Nations and Nationalism*. Oxford: Blackwell, 1983.

Gibbons, Luke, *Transformations in Irish Culture*. Cork: Cork University Press, 1996.

Giddens, Anthony, *Modernity and Self-Identity: Self and Society in the Late Modern Age*. Oxford: Polity, 1991.

Goffman, Erving, *The Presentation of Self in Everyday Life*. New York: Anchor Books, 1959.

Goldring, Maurice, *Pleasant the Scholar's Life: Irish Intellectuals and the Construction of the Nation State*. London: Serif, 1993.

Graves, Robert, and Alan Hodge, *The Long Weekend: A Social History of Great Britain 1918–1939*. London: Faber & Faber, 1991.

Gray, Breda, and Louise Ryan, '(Dis)locating "Woman" and Women in Representations of Irish Nationality', in A. Byrne and M. Leonard (eds.), *Women and Irish Society*. Belfast: Beyond the Pale Publications, 1997.

Gregson, Nicky, and Gillian Rose, 'Taking Butler Elsewhere: Performativities, Spatialities and Subjectivities', *Environment and Planning D: Society and Space*, vol. 18, no. 4, 2000, pp. 433–52.

Groneman, Carol, 'Working-Class Immigrant Women in Mid-Nineteenth-Century New York: The Irish Women's Experience', *Journal of Urban History*, vol. 4, no. 3, May 1978, pp. 255–65.

Hall, Frank, 'Not Irish/Now Irish: Contradictions of Nation and Experience in Expressive Body Movement', paper presented at The Scattering: Ireland and the Irish Diaspora Conference, University College Cork, 25 September 1997.

___, 'Posture in Irish Dancing', *Visual Anthropology*, vol. 8, 1996, pp. 251–66.

___, '"Your Mr Joyce Is a Fine Man: But Have You Seen Riverdance?"', *New Hibernia Review*, vol. 1, no. 3, 1997 pp. 134–42.

___, *Competitive Irish Dance: Art, Sport, Duty*. Madison, Wisconsin: Macater Press, 2008.

Hall, Reginald R., 'Irish Music and Dance in London, 1890–1970: A Socio-Cultural History', unpublished Ph.D. thesis, Sussex University, 1994.

Hall, Stuart, 'Cultural Identity and Diaspora', in J. Rutherford (ed.), *Identity, Community, Culture, Difference*. London: Lawrence and Wishart, 1990, pp. 222–37.

___, 'The Question of Cultural Identity', in Stuart Hall, David Held and Tony McGrew, *Modernity and its Futures*. Cambridge: Polity Press/Open University Press, 1992, pp. 274–316.

___, (ed.), *Representation: Cultural Representations and Cultural Practices*. Sage/Open University Press, 2003.

Hansen, Miriam, 'Chameleon and Catalyst: The Cinema as an Alternative Public Sphere', in G. Turner (ed.), *The Film Cultures Reader*. London: Routledge, 2002, pp. 390–420.

Harris Walsh, Kristin, 'Irish-Newfoundland Step Dancing and Cultural Identity in Newfoundland', *Ethnologies,* vol. 30, no. 1, 2008, pp. 125–40.

Harvey, David, *The Condition of Postmodernity: An Enquiry into the Origins of Cultural Change.* Oxford: Blackwell, 1989.

Hast, Dorothea E., 'Performance, Transformation, and Community: Contra Dance in New England', *Dance Research Journal,* vol. 25, no. 1, 1993, pp. 21–32.

Hendrikson, Carol, 'The Evolution of Irish Step Dance: From Early Irish History to Modern American Tap Dance', *Viltis,* vol. 42, no. 6, 1984, pp. 10–11.

Hobsbawm, E., and Ranger, T. (eds.), *The Invention of Tradition.* Cambridge: Cambridge University Press, 1983.

Ignatiev, Noel, *How the Irish Became White.* London: Routledge, 1995.

Illouz, Eva, *Consuming the Romantic Utopia: Love and the Cultural Contradictions of Capitalism.* Berkeley: University of California Press, 1997.

Inglis, Tom, *Moral Monopoly: The Catholic Church in Modern Irish Society.* Dublin: Gill & Macmillan, 1987.

___, *Moral Monopoly: The Rise and Fall of the Catholic Church in Modern Ireland.* Dublin: University College Dublin Press, 1998.

___, and Katie Liston, Editors' introduction to special issue on sexuality of the *Irish Journal of Sociology,* vol. 12, no. 2, 2003, pp. 3–4.

Jähner, U., '"Ich weis, ich muss noch an mir arbeiten": Über Casting Shows im Fernsehen', *Prokla. Zeitschrift für kritische Sozialwissenschaft,* vol. 35, no. 4, 2005, pp. 619–35.

Jordan-Smith, Paul, '"For as Many as Will"': Deciphering the Folklore of Contra Dance and English Country Dance Events', Ph.D. thesis, University of California, Los Angeles, 2000.

Kavanagh, Donncha, Carmen Kuhling and Kieran Keohane, 'Dance-work: Images of Organization in Irish Dance', *Organization,* vol. 15, no. 5, 2008, pp. 725–42.

Keane, Raymond, in D. Mulrooney (ed.), *Irish Moves: An Illustrated History of Dance and Physical Theatre in Ireland.* Dublin: The Liffey Press, 2006, pp. 197–200.

Kenny, Kevin, *The American Irish: A History.* Harlow: Longman, 2000.

Kimmel, Michael, 'Consuming Manhood: The Feminization of American Culture and the Recreation of the Male Body, 1832–1920', in L. Goldstein (ed.), *The Male Body: Features, Destinies, Exposures.* Ann Arbor: University of Michigan Press, 1994, pp. 12–42.

Kneafsey, Moya, '"If It Wasn't For the Tourists We Wouldn't Have An Audience": The Case of Tourism and Traditional Music in North Mayo', in M. Cronin and B. O'Connor (eds.), *Irish Tourism: Image, Culture and Identity.* Clevedon: Channel View Publications, 2003, pp. 21–42.

Konig, J. 'Irish Traditional Dance-music: A Sociological Study of Its Structure, Development and Functions in the Past and at Present', Ph.D. thesis, University of Amsterdam, 1976.

Kracauer, Siegfried, *The Mass Ornament: Weimar Essays.* Ed. and Trans. Thomas Y. Levin. Cambridge, MA: Harvard University Press, 1995.

Kuhn, Annette, *An Everyday Magic: Cinema and Cultural Memory.* London and New York: I.B. Tauris, 2002.

Lange, R., *The Nature of Dance.* London: MacDonald & Evans, 1975.

Langhamer, Claire, *Women's Leisure in England, 1920–60.* Manchester: Manchester University Press, 2000.

Leonard, Marion, 'Performing Identities: Music and Dance in the Irish Communities of Coventry and Liverpool', *Social and Cultural Geography,* vol. 6, no. 4, 2005, pp. 515–29.

Levinson, Andre, *Andre Levinson: Writings from Paris in the Twenties.* Eds. Joan Acocella and Lynn Garofola. Middleton, Connecticut: Wesleyan University Press, 1991.

MacDonagh, W. Mandle and P. Travers (eds.), *Irish Culture and Nationalism,* 1750–1950. London: Macmillan, 1983.

Mac Fhionnlaoich, Cormac, *Stair na Rinci Gaelacha.* Átha Cliath: An Comisiún le Rincí Gaelacha, 1973.

McAvoy, S., 'The Regulation of Sexuality in the Irish Free State, 1929–35,' in G. Jones and E. Malcolm (eds.), *Medicine, Disease and the State in Ireland 1650–1940.* Cork: Cork University Press, 1999, pp. 253–66.

McGivern, John, interview on *Donncha's Sunday,* RTÉ, Radio One, 27 October, 1985.

McMahon, Timothy G., *Grand Opportunity: The Gaelic Revival and Irish Society, 1893–1910.* Syracuse: Syracuse University Press, 2008.

McNeill, William Hardy, *Keeping Together in Time: Dance and Drill in Human History.* Harvard: Harvard University Press, 1997.

Maguire, Debbie, 'From Radio Reels to Celtic Tiger: The Evolution of Screen Representations of Irish Dance', unpublished M.A. dissertation in Film and Television Studies, Dublin City University, 2008.

Malcolm, Elizabeth, 'Popular Recreation in Nineteenth Century Ireland', in O. Manning, Susan A. *Ecstasy and the Demon: Feminism and Nationalism in the Dances of Mary Wigman.* Berkeley: University of California Press, 1993.

Masero, Angelika, 'The Changes in Irish Dance since Riverdance', B.A. thesis, Western Kentucky University, 2010.

Mauss, M., 'The Techniques of the Body'. Trans. B. Brewster. *Economy and Society,* vol. 2, no. 1, pp. 70–88 (first published in 1934).

Meaney, Geraldine, 'Sex and Nation: Women in Irish Culture and Politics', in A. Smyth (ed.), *Irish Women's Studies Reader.* Dublin: Attic Press, 1993, pp. 230–44.

Memmi, Albert, *The Colonizer and the Colonized*. New York: Orion Press, 1965.

Meyer, Moe, 'Mapping the Body Politic: Embodying Political Geography in Irish Dance', *Performance Research*, vol. 6, no. 2, 2001, pp. 67–74.

___, 'Dance and the Politics of Orality: A Study of the Irish Scoil Rince', *Dance Research Journal*, vol. 27, no. 1, 1995, pp. 25–40.

Miller, Kirby, *Emigrants and Exiles: Ireland and the Irish Exodus to North America*. Oxford: Oxford University Press, 1985.

Moloney, Mick, *Far from the Shamrock Shore: The Story of Irish-American Immigration through Song*. Cork: Collins Press, 2002.

___, J'aime Morrison and Colin Quigley, *Close to the Floor: Irish Dance from the Boreen to Broadway*. Madison WI: Macater, 2008.

Monaghan, Terry, and Mo Dodson, 'Fractured Legacy: Why Did the Irish Contribute so Much to American Tap Dance and so Little to Lindy Hop?', presentation at Dancing on Shannon's Shores Conference, University of Limerick, June 2003.

Morley, David, and Kevin Robins, *Spaces of Identity: Global Media, Electronic Landscapes and Cultural Boundaries*. London: Routledge, 1995.

Mulrooney, Deirdre, *Irish Moves: An Illustrated History of Dance and Physical Theatre in Ireland*. Dublin: The Liffey Press, 2006.

Ní Bhriain, Orfhlaith, 'Irish Dancing, Ethnicity and Cultural Transmission among Post-War Irish Immigrants in Britain: A Case Study from the West Midlands (Birmingham)', paper presented to the XVI European Seminar in Ethnomusicology: John Blacking's Legacy, Queen's University Belfast, 7–10 September 2000.

Nic Eoin, Máirín, 'The Native Gaze: Literary Perceptions of Tourists in the West Kerry Gaeltacht', in Michael Cronin and Barbara O'Connor (eds.), *Irish Tourism: Image, Culture and Identity*. Clevedon: Channel View Publications, 2003, pp. 141–58.

Norris, R. Sachs, 'Embodiment and Community', *Western Folklore*, vol. 60, nos. 2–3, 2001, pp. 111–24.

Novack, Cynthia J., 'The Processes of Perception in Three Dancing Bodies', in *Dance and Meaning: A Communications Approach*. Ed. Diane Freedman. Illinois: University of Illinois Press, 1993.

___, 'The Body's Endeavors as Cultural Practices', in S.L. Foster (ed.), *Choreographing History*. Bloomington: Indiana University Press, 1995, pp. 177–84.

O'Boyle, Neil, *New Vocabularies, Old Ideas: Culture, Irishness and the Advertising Industry*. Bern, Switzerland: Peter Lang, 2011.

Ó Cinnéide, B., *Riverdance: The Phenomenon*. Dublin: Blackhall Press, 2002.

O'Connor, Barbara, 'Women and Media: Social and Cultural Influences on Women's Use of and Response to Television', unpublished Ph.D. thesis, National University of Ireland, 1987.

___, 'Safe Sets: Women, Dance and "Communitas"', in H. Thomas (ed.), *Dance in the City*. Houndmills: Macmillan Press, 1997, pp. 149–72.

___, 'Riverdance', in Michel Peillon and Eamonn Slater (eds.), *Encounters with Modern Ireland: A Sociological Chronicle 1995–1996*. Dublin: Institute of Public Administration, 1998, pp. 51–60.

___, 'Ruin and Romance: Heterosexual Discourses in Irish Popular Dance, 1920–1960', *Irish Journal of Sociology*, vol. 12, no. 2, 2003, pp. 50–67.

___, 'Sexing the Nation: Discourses of the Dancehall in Ireland in the 1930s', *Journal of Gender Studies*, vol. 14, no. 2, 2005, pp. 89–105.

___, 'The Irish Dancing Body, 1920s–1960s', in Deirdre Mulrooney (ed.), *Irish Moves: An Illustrated History of Dance and Physical Theatre in Ireland*. Dublin: Liffey Press, 2006.

___, 'Spaces of Celebrity: National and Global Discourses in the Reception of TV Talent Shows by Irish Teenagers', *Television and New Media*, vol. 13, no. 6, 2012, pp. 568–83.

O'Connor, Nuala, *Bringing It All Back Home: The Influence of Irish Music*. London: British Broadcasting Corporation, 1991.

O'Dowd, Liam, 'Church, State and Women: The Aftermath of Partition', in Chris Curtin, Pauline Jackson and Barbara O'Connor (eds.), *Gender in Irish Society*. Galway University Press, 1987, pp. 3–36.

Ó hAllmhuráin, G., 'Dancing on the Hobs of Hell: Rural Communities in Clare and the Dance Halls Act of 1935', *New Hibernia Review*, vol. 9, no. 4, 2005, pp. 9–18.

O'Keefe, J.G., and A. O'Brien, *A Handbook of Irish Dances*. Dublin: O'Donoghue & Co., 1902.

O'Shea, Helen, *The Making of Irish Traditional Music*. Cork: Cork University Press, 2008.

O'Toole, Fintan, 'Unsuitables from a Distance: The Politics of Riverdance', in *Ex-Isle of Erin: Images of a Global Ireland*. Dublin: New Island Books, 1997, pp. 143–56.

___, 'Perpetual Motion', in P. Brennan and C. de Siant Phalle (eds.), *Arguing at the Crossroads: Essays on a Changing Ireland*. Dublin: New Island Books, 1997.

___, *The Lie of the Land: Irish Identities*. London: Verso, 1999.

___, 'Interview', in D. Theodores (ed.), *Dancing on the Edge of Europe: Irish Choreographers in Conversation*. Cork: Institute for Choreography and Dance, 2003.

Ouellette, Laurie, and James Hay, *Better Living through Reality TV: Television and Post-welfare Citizenship*. Oxford: Blackwell, 2008.

Pearse, Padraig, *An Claidheamh Solais*, 22 May 1909.

Phelan, Peggy, *Unmarked: The Politics of Performance*. London: Routledge, 1993.

Pieterse, Jan Nederveen, 'Globalization as Hybridisation' in Michael Featherstone, Scott Lash and Roland Robertson (eds.), *Global Modernities*. London: Sage, 1995.

Polhemus, Ted, 'Dance, Gender and Culture', in A. Carter (ed.), *The Routledge Dance Studies Reader*. London: Routledge, 1998.

Power, Vincent, *Send 'Em Home Sweatin': The Showbands' Story*. Dublin: Kildanore Press, 1990.

Prickett, Stacey, 'Aerobic Dance and the City: Individual and Social Space', in Helen Thomas (ed.), *Dance in the City*. Houndmills: Macmillan, 1997, pp. 198–217.

Public Dance Halls Act, 1935. Published by the Stationery Office, 1936.

Putnam, Robert D., *Bowling Alone: The Collapse and Revival of American Community*. New York: Simon & Schuster, 2000.

Radcliffe-Brown, A.R., *The Andaman Islanders*. New York: Free Press, 1964.

Rains, Stephanie, *The Irish-American in Popular Culture 1945–2000*. Dublin: Irish Academic Press, 2007.

Rapport, N., and A. Dawson (eds.), *Migrants of Identity: Perceptions of Home in a World of Movement*. Oxford: Berg, 1998.

Robertson, R., 'Glocalization: Time–Space and Homogeneity–Heterogeneity', in Featherstone et al. (eds.), *Global Modernities*, pp. 96–109.

Rockett, Kevin, 'Disguising Dependence: Separatism and Foreign Mass Culture', *Circa*, no. 49, Jan–Feb 1990, pp. 20–25.

Rust, Francis, *Dance in Society*. London: Routledge & Kegan Paul, 1969.

Ruyter, Nancy Lee Chalfa, *The Cultivation of Body and Mind in Nineteenth-Century American Delsartism*. Westport, CT: Greenwood Press, 1999.

Ryan, Louise, 'Negotiating Modernity and Tradition: Newspaper Debates on the Modern Girl in the Irish Free State', *Journal of Gender Studies*, vol. 7, no. 2, 1998, pp. 181–97.

Schiller, Herbert I., *Communication and Cultural Domination*. White Plains, New York: International Arts and Sciences Press, 1976.

Sheehan, John J., *A Guide to Irish Dancing*. London: J. Denvir, 1902.

Silk, M.L., 'Come Downtown and Play', *Leisure Studies*, vol. 26, no. 3, 2007, pp. 253–77.

Sherlock, Joyce I., 'Globalisation, Western Culture and Riverdance', in A. Brah, M. Hickman and M. Mac an Ghaill (eds.), *Thinking Identities: Ethnicity, Racism and Culture*. Basingstoke: Macmillan, 1999, pp. 205–18.

Simmel, Georg, 'The Stranger', in C. Lemert, *Social Theory: The Multicultural and Classic Readings*. Boulder, CO: Westview Press, 2009, pp. 184–89.

Smith, James M., 'The Politics of Sexual Knowledge: The Origins of Ireland's Containment Culture of the Carrigan Report (1931)', *Journal of the History of Sexuality*, vol. 13, no. 2, 2004, pp. 208–233.

Smyth, J., 'Dancing, Depravity, and All That Jazz', *History Ireland*, Summer, 1993, pp. 51–4.

Smyth, Sam, *Riverdance the Story*. London: Andre Deutsch, 1996.

Snape, R., 'Continuity, Change and Performativity in Leisure: English Folk Dance and Modernity 1900–1939', *Leisure Studies*, vol. 28, no. 3, 2009, pp. 297–311.

Stacey, Jackie, *StarGazing: Hollywood Cinema and Female Spectatorship*. London: Routledge, 1994.

Stokes, Martin, *Ethnicity, Identity and Music: The Musical Construction of Place*. Oxford: Berg, 1994.

Tabar, P., 'The Cultural and Affective Logic of the Dabki: A Study of a Lebanese Folkloric Dance in Australia', *Journal of Intercultural Studies*, vol. 26, nos. 1–2, 2005, pp. 139–157.

Thomas, Helen (ed.), *Dance, Gender and Culture*. London: Macmillan, 1993.

___, *Dance, Modernity and Culture: Explorations in the Sociology of Dance*. London: Routledge, 1995.

___, *The Body, Dance and Cultural Theory*. Houndmills: Macmillan, 2003.

___, 'Physical Culture, Bodily Practices and Dance in Late Nineteenth-century and Early Twentieth-century America', *Dance Research*, vol. 22, no. 2, 2004, pp. 185–204.

Toelken, Barrie, 'The Heritage Arts Imperative', *Journal of American Folklore*, vol. 116, 2003, pp. 196–205.

Tomko, Linda J., 'Fete Accompli: Gender, "folk-dance", and Progressive-era Political Ideals in New York City', in S. Leigh Foster (ed.), *Corporalities: Dancing Knowledge, Culture and Power*. London: Routledge, 1996, pp. 155–76.

___, *Dancing Class: Gender, Ethnicity and Social Divides in American Dance, 1890–1920*. Bloomington, IN: Indiana University Press, 1999.

Tomell-Presto, Jessica, 'Performing Irish Identities through Irish Dance', unpublished Ph.D. dissertation, Southern Illinois University, Carbondale, 2003.

Tomlinson, John, *Globalization and Culture*. Cambridge: Polity, 1999.

Tovey, Hilary, and Perry Share, *A Sociology of Ireland*. Dublin: Gill & Macmillan, 2000.

Tubridy, Michael, 'The Set Dancing Revival', *Ceol na hEireann*, no. 2, 1994, pp. 23–35.

Turner, Victor, *Dramas, Fields and Metaphors: Symbolic Action in Human Society*. Ithaca, New York: Cornell University Press, 1974.

___, *From Ritual to Theatre*. New York: PAJ Publications, 1982.

Urry, John, *Consuming Places*. London: Routledge, 1995.

Vallely, Fintan, *Companion to Irish Traditional Music*. (2nd edition). Cork: Cork University Press, 2011.

Veblen, Thorstein, *The Theory of the Leisure Class*. New York: Mentor, 1953 [1899].

Walkowitz, Daniel J. 'The Cultural Turn and a New Social History: Folk Dance and the Renovation of Class in Social History', *Journal of Social History*, Spring, 2006, pp. 781–802.

Wallerstein, Immanuel, 'Culture as the Ideological Background of the Modern World System', in M. Featherstone (ed.), *Global Culture: Nationalism, Globalization and Modernity*. London: Sage, 1991, pp. 31–5.

Ward, Andrew, 'Dancing around Meaning (and the Meaning around Dance)', in H. Thomas (ed.), *Dance in the City*. Houndmills: Macmillan, 1997, pp. 3–20.

Ward, Margaret, *Unmanageable Revolutionaries: Women and Irish Nationalism*. Dingle, Co. Kerry: Brandon, 1983.

Whelan, Kevin, 'The Regional Impact of Irish Catholicism, 1700–1850', in W. Smyth and L.K. Whelan (eds.), *Common Ground: Essays on the Historical Geography of Ireland*. Cork: Cork University Press, 1988.

___, 'The Bases of Regionalism', in Proinsias Ó Drisceoil (ed.), *Culture in Ireland – Regions: Identity and Power*. Proceedings of the Cultures of Ireland Group Conference, 27–29 November 1992. Belfast: The Institute of Irish Studies, 1996, pp. 5–62.

Whyte, J.H., *Church and State in Modern Ireland*. Dublin: Gill & Macmillan, 1971.

Williams, Raymond, *The Country and the City*. London: Chatto & Windus, 1973.

Williams, Rosalind, 'The Dream World of Mass Consumption', in Chandra Mukerji and Michael Schudson (eds.), *Rethinking Popular Culture*. Berkeley: University of California Press, 1991, pp. 198–235.

Wolff, Janet, Foreword to Adair, C. *Women and Dance: Sylphs and Sirens*. New York: New York University Press, 1992.

Wulff, Helena, 'Moving Irish Bodies: Moral Politics, National Identity and Dance', in Noel Dyck and Eduardo P. Archetti (eds.), *Sport, Dance and Embodied Identities*. Oxford: Berg, 2003.

___, 'Memories in Motion: The Irish Dancing Body', *Body & Society*, vol. 11, no. 4, 2005, pp. 45–62.

Wulff, Helena, *Dancing at the Crossroads: Memory and Mobility in Ireland*. New York: Berghahn, 2007.

Young, Arthur, *A Tour of Ireland*. London: Bell, 1892, p. 1446.

Yu-Chen Lin, 'Ireland on Tour: Riverdance, the Irish Diaspora, and the Celtic Tiger', *EurAmerica*, vol. 40, no. 1, 2010, pp. 31–64.

Film and Broadcasting

Ballroom of Romance (1982) Pat O'Connor (dir.), Dublin: Radio Telefís Éireann.

Gangs of New York (2002) Martin Scorsese (dir.), New York: Miramax Films.

Some Mother's Son (1996) Terry George (dir.), Ireland/US: Hell's Kitchen Productions.

The National – A Ballroom of Dreams (2002) Liam Wylie (dir.), Ireland: Campbell Ryan Productions.

Titanic (1997), James Cameron (dir.), Los Angeles, Twentieth Century Fox Film Corporation.

Donncha's Sunday, RTÉ Radio One, 27 October 1985.

Seapoint, *Cead Isteach,* series produced by Scannán Dobharchú. Broadcast on TG4, 25 October 1999.

The Town Hall, Loughrea, on Tom McGurk, RTÉ Radio One, 23 August 2004.

Index

175